TITANIC MEMO

the making of

A NIGHT TO REMEMBER

Acknowledgements

My grateful thanks to the National Maritime Museum and especially to
Alasdair Macleod and Jane Ace for guiding the book through all its stages.
My thanks are also due to my old friend Sir Arthur C. Clarke who has given
me great encouragement with the present book and for his kindness in
providing the preface.

TITANIC MEMORIES
the making of
A NIGHT TO REMEMBER

William MacQuitty

Dedicated to the craftsmen and creative artists who
overcame daunting odds to turn Walter Lord's superb
book *A Night to Remember* into a great film.

*For
Ann & Morrie
With all good wishes and
Many Happy Memories.
Bill
30th September 2002*

First published in 2000 by the
National Maritime Museum
Greenwich, London, SE10 9NF

ISBN 0 948065 36 2

Printed and bound in the UK by
Westway Offset Limited

Front cover: Criterion Theatre on Broadway.
Ken Hargreaves, president of Rank Film Distributors of America,
William MacQuitty, producer, and Geoffrey Martin,
the Rank US publicity chief prepare for the opening night.

Back cover: one of the special effects created for the film.

Contents

7   Preface

8   Launchings

13   Locations and obstructions

17   Set to work

19   Truth to tell

23   The final cut

26   Convincing the Americans

29   Probing the depths

30   The never-ending voyage

33   London première programme

47   Producer's shooting diary

A Night to Remember Cast List

Lightoller	KENNETH MORE	Boxhall	JACK WATLING
Mr Clarke	RONALD ALLEN	Evans	GEOFFREY BAYLDON
Peuchen	ROBERT AYRES	Moody	MICHAEL BRYANT
Mrs Lucas	HONOR BLACKMAN	Q M Rowe	CYRIL CHAMBERLAIN
Captain Rostron	ANTHONY BUSHELL	Gallagher	RICHARD CLARKE
Murphy	JOHN CAIRNEY	Mrs Farrell	BEE DUFFELL
Mrs Clarke	JILL DIXON	Guggenheim	HAROLD GOLDBLATT
Mrs Lightoller	JANE DOWNS	3rd Officer (Carpathia)	GERALD HARPER
Col. Gracie	JAMES DYRENFORTH	Victualling Manager	RICHARD HAYWARD
Andrews	MICHAEL GOODLIFFE	3rd Steward	THOMAS HEATHCOTE
Phillips	KENNETH GRIFFITH	Polish Mother	DANUTA KARELL
Lady Richard	HARRIETTE JOHNS	Engineer Officer Hesketh	ANDREW KEIR
Chairman	FRANK LAWTON	Polish Girl	CHRISTINA LUBICZ
Murdoch	RICHARD LEECH	Gibson	BARRY MacGREGOR
Bride	DAVID McCALLUM	Steward No 5	EDDIE MALIN
Cottam	ALEC McCOWAN	Mr Farrell	PATRICK McALINNEY
Mrs Brown	TUCKER McGUIRE	Mrs Straus	HELEN MISENER
Lucas	JOHN MERIVALE	Kate	MARY MONAHAN
Yates	RALPH MICHAEL	Lowe	HOWARD PAYS
Captain Smith	LAURENCE NAISMITH	Clergyman (Carpathia)	PHILIP RAY
Captain Lord	RUSSELL NAPIER	Stone	HAROLD SIDDONS
Hoyle	REDMOND PHILLIPS	Mr Bull	JULIAN SOMERS
Joughin	GEORGE ROSE	Groves	TIM TURNER
Dr O'Loughlin	JOSEPH TOMELTY	Mr Straus	MEIER TZELNIKER
Sir Richard	PATRICK WADDINGTON		

Dear Bill,

Allow me to take this opportunity to express my thanks ... as your vision to create the film "A Night to Remember" has had a ripple effect through modern culture, manifesting itself most recently in my own film 'Titanic', inspired in part by your film. You have my gratitude and my best wishes for a wonderful Christmas and a rewarding New Year.

Wishing you a beautiful Holiday Season and a New Year of Peace and Happiness

Message from James Cameron, Director of Academy Award™ winning film *Titanic* to William MacQuitty.

Preface

A popular term in modern physics is 'entanglement' - the mysterious influence of one nuclear particle on another, for no apparent reason. Well, all my life I seem to have been entangled with the *Titanic*, which sank five years before I was born.

The very first story I ever wrote was called 'Icebergs of Space' and concerned an interplanetary liner which collided with an asteroid. The big surprise in the last line was the name of the spaceship, you'll never guess ...

I am happy to say this piece of juvenilia was destroyed long ago, but now we know that there really *are* 'icebergs' in space, because many comets consist largely of frozen water. Only recently has it been appreciated that they can be a serious menace: one wiped out the dinosaurs 65 million years ago. Although Spaceship Earth, unlike the *Titanic* is indeed unsinkable, it's certainly not invulnerable, and in June 1999 the House of Lords discussed my concept of 'Project Spaceguard' to establish a planetary warning system. *Titanic* was lost because of a pair of missing binoculars: could our civilization be destroyed because there aren't enough telescopes to watch the sky?

To continue with my own entanglement, in *Imperial Earth* (1976) I raised the *Titanic* and sailed her to New York harbour. We now know that this can't happen because the ship is in two badly damaged portions. So later, in *The Ghost from the Grand Banks* (1990), I exploited the situation that actually exists, and the dedication read as follows:

For my old friend Bill MacQuitty -

who, as a boy,
witnessed the launch of R.M.S. *Titanic,*
and, forty-five years later,
sank her for the second time.

Although there have been many films about the *Titanic* culminating recently in James Cameron's brilliant box-office triumph, nothing will ever surpass Bill's *A Night to Remember* which remains one of the best British films ever made. No small part for the success was due to the superb cameraman Geoffrey Unsworth, who later moved from sea to space, when he shot *2001* for Stanley Kubrick - thus in a sense closing the cycle I began as a small boy.

Why did this maritime disaster - by no means the worst because thousands have perished in other wrecks - haunt the last century, as it will doubtless continue to haunt the new? There are many reasons: it has the classic perfection of a Greek tragedy with its theme of man against the gods. And now it has been matched by two other chilling examples of technological disasters unimaginable in 1912 - Chernobyl and *Challenger*. There will be others in this new millennium.

And now some final entanglements. The role of perhaps the most tragic character, the ship's designer Thomas Andrews, was played by Michael Goodliffe - whose father Arnold was headmaster at Huish Grammar School and thus a major influence on my own life. Seventy years later I can still recall my excitement when he proved to our maths class that the sum of the cubes of the first n integers equals the square of their sum. I still think this is an astonishing fact.

Finally: just a few hours after I received the manuscript of *Titanic Memories* I switched on local TV - and there was the wreck on the seabed, while the sound carried the voice of Fourth Officer Joseph Boxhall, who Bill thanks for crucial advice on the movie because, 'He had been on deck when the ship struck the iceberg and continued to be at the heart of the rescue operation until she sank.'

Can anyone tell me what's going on here?

Arthur C. Clarke May 2000

Launchings

I was born in Belfast on 15 May 1905, which meant I was just past my sixth birthday when the *Titanic* was launched on 30 May 1911. The spectacle of her huge hull rising above the slipway at the Harland & Wolff shipyard as the work of the shipbuilders progressed had provided my childhood with one of its most vividly remembered sights. The *Titanic* was, as all Belfast and the rest of the world knew, going to be the largest, best-designed and most beautiful ship ever to sail the high seas. It was beyond me, as a frail frightened little boy, plagued by asthma and bronchitis, to imagine how this huge mountain of metal could ever be floated, but my ancestors had provided me with my greatest asset: an enormous curiosity and persistence.

My father took me to the launch. The day was glorious and the sun shone from a clear sky. The smell of the sea mingled with the smells of the shipyard, where a vast throng of workers and spectators waited in awed silence. Suddenly a rocket flamed into the sky, the chocks were knocked away, hydraulic rams pushed and the huge vessel began to move down the slipway, very slowly at first, then faster and faster. It dragged the mounds of restraining anchor chains along the ground. A great wave rose as her stern hit the sea. The noise was thunderous. All the ships in Belfast harbour sounded their sirens, the vast crowd cheered, the hull was buoyed up by the water. My fears vanished. This great ship had been built by people like me. What they could do I would also be able to do in time. I too was an Ulsterman. My heart swelled with pride.

On 2 April the following year I saw the fitted-out *Titanic* as she sailed away to begin her maiden voyage. Before her lay the freedom of the oceans and I longed to be aboard. The news of her

William MacQuitty 15ᵗʰ May 1911

tragic fate twelve days later shocked the world. The inheritance of Victorian certainty was shattered and something had changed for ever. Worst hit were the people of Ulster, all of whom had links with the ship, through relatives, friends or the men who built her. It came as a dreadful shock to me as it did for everyone else, but I absorbed the basic lesson: time was the most precious gift of life and death was for all of us.

At the age of eight I was sent to my first boarding school, with a new cabin trunk carefully packed with my school clothes. It seemed a good omen: the beginning of a voyage, with the same mixture of apprehension and excitement. Sadly, however, the world was already forgetting the *Titanic*. In 1914 it began to have to cope with a new kind of war. Yet while triumph and disaster, Kipling's 'two impostors', came to characterize so much of the century as it went along my personal links with the ship seemed to deepen. It was as if there were a debt that I might be able to repay one day. I could never imagine how this might come about.

I saw the fitted-out *Titanic* as she sailed away to begin her maiden voyage

As my adult life began, my work took me first to the Far East as a banker. I travelled the world and learnt to work at things I liked. By the time the Second World War broke out I was back in London, working in film production for the Ministry of Information. I recorded the Blitz, the war artists, the VE Day celebrations, and also filmed the reconstruction of the bombed city of Plymouth. I never did have a fear of changing jobs, and I was even less afraid of failing to succeed at them. Even in my nineties, I still have an overwhelming desire to prove anyone wrong who says something cannot be done.

The example of my *Titanic* experience had helped to guide me through many of life's stormy waters when I finally reached a haven in 1951 and had the good fortune to marry Betty Bastin, the beautiful president of the students' union at the London School of Economics. We had three children, and when in 1956 she returned from hospital with the third, Miranda, she also had with her a review of a book about the *Titanic* by an author who had spent twenty years meticulously researching what really happened to the ship. The book was Walter Lord's now famous *A Night to Remember*, and when I read it I realized it was exactly what I had so long been waiting for. I obtained an option on the film rights, and Walter came to see me. It was a moment of instant mutual approval and we became life-long friends. To see how the book might be made into a film, we went through it detail by detail with mounting enthusiasm. We had no doubts about the importance of this project. Walter had loaded the cannon. It was my job to hit the target.

The most important thing that a film producer needs is a first-class

Queen's Road, Belfast with shipyard men leaving work. RMS *Titanic* in background. Photograph dated May 1911.

story. This I had found. Next he needs finance, a studio and distribution. I had just completed a film called *The Black Tent* for the Rank Organization. It was a Western Desert romance made on location in Libya in August in the hottest spot on earth. We had shot it in wide-screen Vista-Vision, in the crystal-clear glowing colour beloved by the distributors. It had cost some £250,000. The film about the *Titanic* which we planned to be in small-screen black and white, was going to cost double that. I went to see John Davis, Rank's managing director, in his office at Pinewood Studios.

John had been the chief accountant to Odeon Theatres since the late 1930s and after J. Arthur Rank bought the chain in 1942 he remained with the organization. He was a very tough operator who rarely hesitated to fire anyone who failed to produce a profit. He had got rid of so many people and talents, even including his own board members, that they formed a club called the 'Rank Outsiders'. The result was that he was feared and hated. Nevertheless I liked him. Operating in a sea of deceit, he was straight and he kept his word.

'Why do you want to make this film?' he barked. 'It's been made

'Why do you want to make this film?' he barked. 'It's been made before.'

before. And why do you want to buy the book and give the writer two and a half per cent of the profits? The story's in the public domain. Why do you want to make it in small-screen black and white when you know the distributors want wide-screen colour?' His advisers and department heads nodded assent. 'It's just another shipwreck,' he insisted, 'on which you want to spend half a million.'

The Belfast *Titanic* memorial in its original location at Donegal Square North.

'John', I said, 'it's not another shipwreck. It's the end of an era.'

'None of your Irish blarney,' he retorted. 'Tell me the truth.'

'To start with,' I began, 'it was an age of arrogance. Stateroom passengers, to establish their wealth, paid £875 for the five-day crossing Southampton to New York. Steerage passengers paid £12. In Belfast, the names on the Titanic Memorial are in order of importance, while those on

the nearby 1914-18 war memorial are in alphabetical order. This will be the true story of the sinking.

Previous films have only used the disaster as a vehicle for stars, or, as in the German version, for propaganda. In this film the ship will be the star. The tragedy has more human emotion than star actors could ever produce. There were 1,503 people who died, 705 were saved.'

After a moment's silence Davis gave instructions to call the Belfast office and have them check out my account of the memorials. 'Who do you want to direct this film?' he asked.

'Roy Baker,' I said.

'But,' said Davis, 'he's eight weeks overdue on *The One That Got Away.*'

'He'll be on time with this one, provided no one interferes,' I said firmly.

I thought I caught the glimmer of a smile. There was a long pause, before, with a serious look at me, he said, 'Make it.' I think the challenge had appealed to him. 'Have you anything

Alexander Vetchinsky, the film's Art Director, surrounded by the plans of the ship.

more to tell me before you go?' he asked.

'Well,' I said, 'only that as I was on my way over I heard on the car radio that the bank rate has gone up two and a half per cent, but I expect you knew that.'

'If I'd known it, you wouldn't have got the contract.' He started to smile, stood up and we shook hands.

Storyboard sketches used to decide exactly what was required before setting up difficult shots.

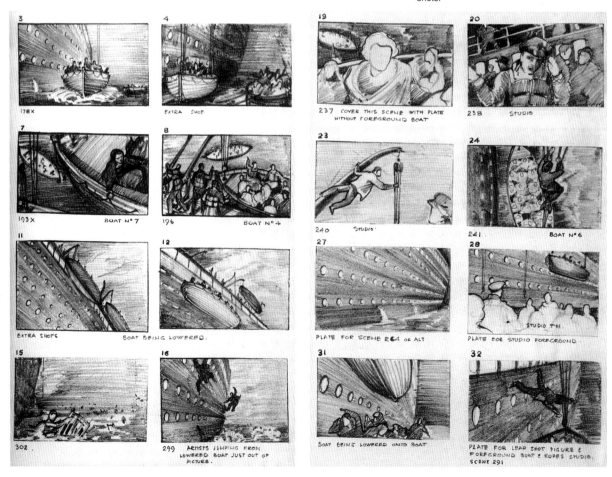

Cast and Crew

Among the several earlier films featuring the *Titanic* story, the first, *Saved from the Titanic* was made in the same year the disaster happened. It starred Miss Dorothy Gibson, one of the survivors. *Atlantic*, a British-German dual-language version of 1929, was the first British talkie to have a soundtrack throughout. The wholly German wartime version of 1943 was a vehicle for Dr Goebbels' anti-British spleen. More recently, in 1953, the Twentieth Century-Fox production, *Titanic*, had tacked an emotional melodrama on to the historic facts, with Clifton Webb and Barbara Stanwyck playing the lead roles. My idea that the ship should be the star was an entirely new approach.

For my director I was fortunate to get Roy Baker. He was a brilliant artist with a great sense of period. We agreed that the film would start quite simply with the launch and continue chrono-

Director Roy Baker discusses a scene with actor Laurence Naismith who played the part of Captain Edward J Smith.

logically until the end. It required a first-rate scriptwriter, one who could weave a seamless web out of Walter's book of hundreds of characters and situations - a sack of pearls that needed threading. Roy suggested Eric Ambler, the author of such classic thrillers as *The Mask of Dimitrios*, with whom he had served in the Army Film Unit during the war. Eric had shown he had

equal skills in scriptwriting, as in his treatment of the film version of Nicholas Monsarrat's *The Cruel Sea*. He seemed the ideal choice and, luckily for us, he was free and keen to take on the screenplay.

As Eric got down to the writing, Roy and I checked each scene to see that it presented no filming problems. Where there were possible difficulties we had sketches drawn. Finally a superb script emerged. When we complimented Eric on his

Captain Edward J Smith played in the film by Laurence Naismith.

acute observation and sparkling text, he simply said, 'Everything was in the book. All I had to do was knit it together.'

Next came the cast. There were forty-nine speaking parts and many of the hundreds of extras had lines. We were not looking for stars, but for actors who could represent real people. Stars would have been unreal. Kenneth More, however, was an immediate choice for the part of Second Officer Charles Herbert Lightholler, and there was no denying he was a star name in British cinema after his success in the vintage car comedy *Genevieve* and most recently his depiction of the war hero Douglas Bader in *Reach for the Sky*. We were therefore doubtful whether he was likely to accept a part that would have him on screen for only some twenty minutes. Roy caught up with him in the United States, where he was publicizing the Bader film. Would he be interested in *A Night to Remember*?, asked Roy. 'Yes, indeed,' replied

Kenneth, who was immediately drawn towards the project. As he wrote in his autobiography *More or Less* 'All the coincidences of life which have fascinated me since boyhood were here encapsulated in one story.'

We were lucky with the rest of the casting, too, and assembled a group of actors with a wide range of abilities, especially in character roles. Many were equally well-known for their work both on stage and in the cinema. Among them were Frank Lawton, the husband of Evelyn Laye; Michael Goodliffe and Alec McCowen, who both had distinguished careers in classical theatre; David McCallum, who was graduating from acting neurotic teenagers and beginning to receive wider recognition; Jill Dixon, who had played in Shakespeare as well as in three of the Norman Wisdom comedy films; and Honor Blackman, who had yet to become a household name as Cathy Gale, the original female lead opposite Patrick McNee, in the famous television series *The Avengers*. She gave a cameo performance of assured dignity as the mother of three children. Above all, there was Laurence Naismith, who was able to bring more than a touch of authenticity to his characterization of the ill-fated Captain Edward J. Smith. Before becoming an actor he had spent two years at sea as a cabin boy. His approach to the role was to study every scrap of information he could find on the real Captain Smith, aware, as he said, that playing someone who was remembered by many still alive was one of the toughest assignments an actor could face.

Vetchinsky checking progress on the lower section of the replica hull.

Detailed technical plans recreated the magnificent staterooms.

The Pinewood art director was Alex Vetchinsky, known as 'Vetch'. He had been famous as a film craftsman since the 1930s for his characterful sets, which were full of entertaining detail. This time there was not much he would need to dream up from his fertile imagination. From the beginning he had blueprints of the *Titanic*, so was never in doubt. He would need to build the centre third of the ship in a way that showed two funnels and four lifeboats. The bow and stern would then have to be built separately as they had to be able to 'sink'.

First, he built a vast concrete foundation to carry the weight of the ship on which the crowd scenes would be shot. The construction had to look correct in every detail. It also had to be solid and able to accept the lowering and raising of lifeboats and, when the last boat had gone, the surging mass of hundreds of terrified people. The ship had to slope gradually from the level to a series of steeper angles. To achieve this effect it was necessary to build the set at a certain angle. Then, by tilting the camera, the deck could be made visually level or else seem to have taken on a more acute angle. Each page of the shooting script clearly showed the angle of the ship for that particular scene. Many of the scenes, of course, would not be shot in sequence. Besides this, all the great staterooms had to be built on platforms underneath which hydraulic jacks would be able to tilt them to match the angles of the deck.

The lifeboats and the davits had to be the same as the *Titanic's*

Vetch was a stout, impatient man with no time for any sort of interference in his domain. The ship became fixed in his mind and he could instantly recognize any mistake, however small, to his well prepared plans. He was a joy to work with and his wants were few: cigars

Notes for Individual Action **Lifeboat Replica**

In one of the most appalling shipping disasters in history a young ship's officer saved his life by clinging on to an overturned collapsible lifeboat. Forty-five years later, his boatbuilder son built an exact replica of the lifeboat for a film about his father.

At 2.20 am on April 15th, 1912, the mighty passenger liner *Titanic* sank in the North Atlantic. Almost 1,500 men, women and children – all those unable to get into the too few lifeboats – were left floating in lifejackets amid the freezing ice-floes.

Almost all perished. A few lucky ones clung with frozen fingers to an overturned collapsible lifeboat which the crew had been unable to launch and had floated off the great ship as she disappeared.

Among those lucky few was the gallant Second Officer of the *Titanic*, Charles Lightoller.

During their new production, "A Night to Remember", which tells the story of the ill-fated *Titanic*, Pinewood Studios asked Col. R T Lightoller, of Staines, Middlesex, the Managing Director of a Thames boatyard, to build an exact replica of the lifeboat his father clung on to.

Col. Lightoller's firm built the boat from drawings located by Captain Leonard Townsend, an ex-Merchant Service officer who is now employed in the film industry and who was responsible for obtaining the material and 'props' used in the film.

Playing the part of Second Officer Lightoller in the film is Kenneth More. Producer of "A Night to Remember", which is based on Walter Lord's best selling book, is William MacQuitty. Direction is by Roy Baker.

An extract from the publicity folder for *A Night to Remember*.

Bill Warrington was in charge of special effects and used this exact scale model to re-create the sinking.

and Turkish baths.

Special effects came under the control of William Warrington. His was the most difficult work. He made a meticulously exact model of the *Titanic*, designed to be shown with lights blazing as it steamed through a quiet sea. At the end it would be seen sinking, with electrically controlled seamen pulling away from the ship in lifeboats. The figures were only four

inches high, but those magnificent last moments turned out to be the most moving in the entire film. They were achieved by manual means, though today the same effects could easily be produced on screen by a computer graphics program.

Finally among the leaders of the production team there was the cameraman, Geoffrey Unsworth. He had worked on my previous film, *The Black Tent*, and now was both free and happy to wind back down from working on wide-screen Panavision to tackle the intense realism of small-screen black and white. The realism he imparted to the scenes he shot were a vital contribution. They still help to define *A Night to Remember* as the most realistic film of the *Titanic* tragedy.

Night filming of the starboard side of the *Asturias* on Clydeside.

Locations and Obstructions

The first location shots were the most important in the film. They were to show the lowering of the lifeboats filled with passengers down the side of the *Titanic* into the sea. They needed to be shot at night from a ship with the same colours as the *Titanic*. The lifeboats and the davits had to be the same as the *Titanic's*. There had to be extras in period costumes. The whole scene would be lit by arc lights powered by generators on anchored barges. The whole operation was going to have to be shot on three nights.

The daunting task that faced us went as follows. The line whose colours matched the *Titanic* was the Shaw Savill and her davits were the same. We were promised the use of one of their ships during a weekend when it was in the Port of London at the Royal Albert Dock between voyages to South Africa. Meanwhile I

Illustration demonstrating the height of the *Titanic* and the drop of the lifeboats.

bought lifeboats identical to those of the *Titanic* from the *Franconia*, which was being broken up. These were on their way from Scotland by road and shooting was due to begin on a Friday.

On Thursday a very embarrassed Shaw Savill port captain telephoned me to say that the line's chairman had decided against the film. Permission to use one of his ships had therefore been withdrawn. Later I heard that the chairman was a friend of the Ismay family. This sensitivity could be accounted for by the fact that the Ismays were closely linked to the *Titanic* story through their interests in the White Star Line. The ship itself had been the fulfilment of the vision of J. Bruce Ismay as managing director of White Star. Subsequently, having survived the disaster, he came in for public criticism for what was seen as his erratic behaviour during the emergency of the sinking.

I tried other companies, but the word had gone about that sinking ships was bad for business. When I asked Lloyds they suggested Thomas

Ward, the Clyde shipbreakers. I caught a plane the same day and flew to Helensburgh. They were breaking up the *Asturias*, which had the same davits as the *Titanic*. The port side was already being broken up, but the starboard side, next to the sea, was still intact. It was perfect for our purposes. By fixing a mirror on the camera, and ensuring that all lettering was then written backwards, we could also transform it into the port side without difficulty.

I asked the manager how much he would charge to allow us to film the starboard side at night only, which would not interfere with his work. He liked the idea and accepted a hundred pounds for ten nights. I asked for a receipt and a signed agreement. Then I warned him that he might be getting a call from the London shipping companies. Sure enough, a telegram arrived the next day, telling him to have no dealings with MacQuitty. The manager only laughed and told me to carry on. 'Just let me know what you want,' he said. 'We'll try to help.'

The *Asturias* had been on the Australia run and was painted white.

A lifejacket – copied for the film.

Glasgow art students came to the rescue and painted it black. The stunt men were to be paid a pound a foot for the eighty-foot drop into the icy waters of the Clyde, and the property department had supplied them with original heavy cork lifejackets. Fortunately I arrived in time to get these changed before any jumps took place. The lifejackets would have broken the stunt men's necks as they hit the water.

Kapok was substituted for cork and all was well.

The lifeboat scenes were shot in December on Ruislip reservoir, not far from the studios. Today it is a boating lake. The water was four feet deep and very cold. This had the advantage of showing up the actors' breath.

> ## The lifejackets would have broken the stunt men's necks as they hit the water

There was no time to allow for any changes of their period clothes between shots, so a drying room was improvised, using powerful hot-air blowers, the normal task of which was to dry out new buildings. I would like to think that those few minutes of respite in an intense heat made a return to the boats almost enjoyable, but Kenneth More retained graphic memories that he expressed in *More or Less*:

'I leaped. Never have I experienced such intense cold in all my life. It was

Checking a kapok-filled lifejacket.

like jumping into a deep freeze. The shock forced the breath out of my body. My heart seemed to stop beating. I felt crushed, unable to think. I had *rigor mortis* without the *mortis* ... We struck out for the boats, struggling and kicking anyone who got in our way. We weren't acting. We were desperate to be rescued. There were eight lifeboats, which would carry about sixty-four each. This meant that

more than 500 men and women in overcoats and fur coats, were threshing about in the lido for quite a long time before they could all haul themselves aboard the boats.'

The final location was to be a simple shot of Harland & Wolff's shipyards. The chairman of the company was Sir Frederick Rebbeck. I knew the family and had been best man at his younger son's wedding, and Sir Frederick had frequently asked me

Kenneth More drenches himself before being filmed in the collapsible lifeboat.

to make a film in Ulster. I went to see him, confident that the project would receive his blessing. He had already heard about my plans and instead he was furious. 'You surely don't intend to make money out of this tragedy!' he roared. 'You can make it in a hundred years' time when all the relatives are dead.'

I tried every ploy to calm the waters. There would be no implications that there had been anything wrong with the beautifully built ship, I explained. Her sister ship the *Olympic* built to the same design, had completed her long life without mishap. The film would show the courage of the passengers and crew. It was a heroic story that deserved to be told.

Sir Frederick's eldest son, Dr Denis, was even more angry than his father, and his reply was even stronger: 'Neither you nor your film crew will be allowed to photograph the shipyard or anything in it,' he declared. 'We will

Filming the lifeboats on Ruislip reservoir near Pinewood Studios

not help you in any way.'

It was sad news for me, but at least I had access to the few surviving shipyard workers who had helped to build the *Titanic*. Over the next couple of weeks I interviewed them. All were helpful and confirmed the high level of skills that had been needed. They also spoke of their life of anxious waiting outside the shipyard gates each morning hoping to be chosen when the foreman picked out the men he

wanted for that day's work. It was a question of no work no pay, and if you were Catholic your chances were slim. If there were no ships under construction, the yard simply closed in the interim.

Our appeals for authentic information on the building of the *Titanic* had produced one response that illustrated sectarian tensions:

Dear Sir,
In your quest for information about the *Titanic*. I wonder if you were told that the Orange men employed in the Belfast ship yard cursed the Pope with Every Rivet they put in the *Titanic* and her registered number 390904 when read from the

back of the paper it was put on was NO POPE. With this so called unsinkable ship the Curse of Almighty God fell on Her and I wonder what they said when they Heard that the Band played *Nearer My God to Thee* as she sank.

The curious thing was that, if you wrote the number down on a piece of paper and turned it backwards to the light, the number seen from the reverse side did seem to read as the correspondent claimed.

Among the men I met who had worked on the *Titanic,* the riveters were in fact the most interesting. Shipbuilding is a great art. First the keel is laid, and from the keel branch ribs that are covered with large sheets of iron, the edges of the iron being drilled with holes for the rivets. These will eventually join the plates together to make a seamless skin of iron. The plates overlap so that the rivet holes coincide. Next the heater boy plucks a white-hot rivet out of his fire and slides

15

it along a metal strip to the tongs of the catch boy. He, in turn, passes the rivet to the holder-on, whose job it is to put it in the hole while a pair of riveters hammer it in swift alternating blows, one being left-handed and the other right-handed. They hammer at tremendous

It took 3 million rivets to sheath the *Titanic*

speed until the rivet is smoothly shaped. As it cools, the rivet contracts, binding the plates together with enormous strength. It took 3 million rivets to sheath the *Titanic*.

I then asked the painter about his work. 'The first-class cabins got three undercoats and four topcoats of paint. Many of the painters chewed tobacco, which they shaved off compressed blocks. When they were doing the last coat they put sawdust in their pockets and spat into the sawdust so that no tobacco spittle splashed the paint. 'What happens today?' I asked. 'Today,' he said, 'it's the "Moon Men". They come in with plastic globes on their heads and spray anything that doesn't move.'

I returned to Pinewood downcast at my failure to film at Harland & Wolff. My desk was filled with work. 'Best look at this first,' said my secretary, Genia Kaye. 'John Davis is worried about it.' She passed me a cutting from the *Manchester Guardian* of 1 November 1957, headlined:

'PUBLICITY – UNCONSCIOUS':

In the ordinary way of business some details are coming out of the care the Rank Organization is taking to make its film of the '*Titanic*' disaster, 'A Night to Remember', as authentic as the book itself. One point that will probably not be emphasized by the publicity men. Harland & Wolff, of Belfast, who built the '*Titanic*', would give no help in the making of the film. I learned this a couple of weeks ago from Dr Denis Rebbeck, a director of the firm, standing on a high tower overlooking the whole of Queen's Island. He pointed out the slip on which the '*Titanic*' was built and exploded into baffled anger at the recollection that Rank had asked permission to use it in making 'A Night to Remember'.

"Too many people from this shipyard lost their lives that night and too many others as well. Why should we help to make an entertainment out of it?"

I sent the following reply to the editor of the *Manchester Guardian* and the paper printed it on 5 November:

Sir, - In today's issue your London Correspondent reports a meeting between Dr Denis Rebbeck and himself, in which Dr Rebbeck, who is a director of Harland & Wolff, of Belfast, the firm who built the *Titanic*, said that 'Too many from this shipyard lost their lives that night and too many others as well. Why should we help to make a film out of it?' I am a Belfast man myself and with many others watched the '*Titanic*' on her trials. When I decided to make this picture I interviewed men of Harland & Wolff who had worked on the '*Titanic*', and I have also spoken to all the survivors available, and have been in correspondence with several hundred people whose relatives were lost on this ship. None of these people suggested that the film should not be made and all were most eager for an accurate account to be given. Dr Rebbeck objects that this great story is being made 'for Entertainment.' I am hoping, Sir, to present the facts accurately; and this is surely sometimes the business of the film-maker, just as it is of the journalist.

Not long afterwards, at the end of what had been a long day, my wonderful secretary Genia handed me a little box, saying, 'This will cheer you up.'

I opened the box. Inside it, wrapped up in newspaper, was a small metal purse. I opened the purse. Inside was a letter from an address in Belfast and an American cent piece. The letter read:

Dear Mr MacQuitty,

Notes for Individual Action **They saw iceberg that killed 1,502 people**

High in the crow's nest of the mighty R.M.S. *Titanic*, lookout men Frederick Fleet and Reginald Lee peered into the night.

The night sky blazed with stars. It was calm, clear and freezing cold. The Atlantic was as smooth as glass. This was the fifth night of the *Titanic's* maiden voyage from Southampton to New York.

Below, in the luxurious staterooms, smoke rooms and restaurants, were some of the richest people on earth. But they meant very little to Fleet and Lee, the 'eyes' of the great ship. On this particular night of 14ᵗʰ April, 1912, they had both been warned to watch out for icebergs.

Their watch was now almost over. They had seen nothing unusual. The *Titanic* raced through the night at 22 knots. The time was just on 11.40 pm.

Suddenly, Fleet saw an object directly ahead. Every second it grew bigger and closer. He immediately gonged the crow's nest bell three times and at the same time, grabbed the telephone and rang the bridge.

"What did you see?" asked a calm voice at the other end.

"Iceberg right ahead", replied Fleet.

"Thank you", said the calm voice and the telephone was placed into its cradle.

For the next few seconds Fleet and Lee stood watching the great iceberg draw nearer. Soon they were almost on top of it when the ship's bow started to swing to port. At the last second it swung clear and the iceberg glided along the starboard side.

It looked to Fleet and Lee like a very near miss. But it did not miss – 300 feet of the mighty liner's underbelly had been ripped out. In exactly 2 hours and forty minutes the ship was to sink and over 1,500 people were to lose their lives.

Fleet and Lee were saved. They were rescued by the liner *Carpathia* and eventually returned to their homes in Southampton.

An extract from the publicity folder for *A Night to Remember*.

I have enclosed a souvenir which you may be interested in, and you may keep it as a gift from me, seeing that you are interested in the loss of the *Titanic*.

I am getting along to 74 years old, and my old bottom ends (legs) are troubling me and I am holed in during the winter months. As to this gift I will give you the facts how l came into possession of the purse, on the page attached to this letter. In conclusion I could not think of anyone that I could leave it to but yourself. All my friends have passed on, most to Davy Jones' locker.

So adios,

An old friend

Sgd. Joe Mulholland

PS. I am one of the Square Riggers before going into steam.

Details

I met an old ship mate of mine down on the River Plate, S.A., La Plata, when ashore on the booze, his name was Baker,

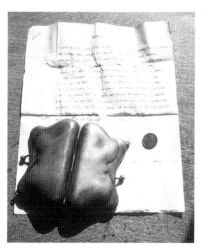

The metal purse, one-cent piece and letter written by Mulholland to MacQuitty.

but all his mates called him Pancake (nickname). He was one of the *Titanic* crew and was one of the lucky ones to get saved. He told me that this purse was lying in the bow of the lifeboat in which he was fortunate to crawl on board. Inside the purse was a brooch and 20

dollars, a ring (signet), one-cent piece, a silver chain attached to the purse as a strap or handle. I asked him what he did with the ring, brooch and purse chain and he told me he flogged them for booze. I got the purse containing one cent from him for a drink or two. Pancake died in the asylum in Belfast.

'This,' said Genia, 'is the 310th reply we have had from Ulster to our letter in the press.'

Although difficult to prove the authenticity of the artefact I was greatly moved...

Set to work

During the time we were filming locations, the huge indoor sets were being built at Pinewood Studios. It was Rank's twenty-first birthday, but *A Night to Remember* was the only film being made. Happily it required all the 1,200 work force and no one needed to be laid off. For the first time at Pinewood everyone was working on the same production.

Our filming began in earnest. For a producer the camera is like a hungry animal requiring continuous feeding. If the film stopped rolling then costs escalated and alarm bells started to ring in the Rank Organization. It was also essential to have alternative sets ready to bypass any emergency, such as rain or snow. Fortunately the special effects unit was safely housed and continued its complicated work immune to the weather, though with much trial and error. Quality had to come first, whatever the cost.

Each morning Genia had all the day's schedules ready: call sheets for actors, timetables for filming, contracts, publicity and running costs. These were dealt with in order of urgency. Contracts were of prime importance. Those for the lead actors were very complicated and occupied many pages of closely written detail. Everything had to be agreed and then countersigned by the producer. Extended time was limited and if extra time was needed the charges and penalties could be enormous. It was easy to run overtime and find you needed a leading actor for an extra day or two. But then the actor might be contracted to another film among other complications. Even one extra day might cost a fortune. From time to time, knowing everything that was in the small print, I was greatly worried, but Hugh Parton, who ran the Pinewood contract department, was a

tower of strength and reassurance, and nothing serious happened.

The variety of problems was endless. An actor had failed to turn up, special props were delayed. Above all, where were we to find engines of the right period in working condition? Fortunately I discovered a disused pumping station at Cricklewood in north London whose 1905 engines were still in order. I arranged to have them restarted and fitted the room with watertight doors. The machinery was correct for the period and Vetch was enthusiastic.

A particular help with speeding up production was the huge mobile crane we had hired to move heavy objects around on the set for the ship. Its driver, Michael Fagan, was resourceful, a small, light and wiry man who impressed me with his eagerness. He could speed up the high ladder to his lofty perch in seconds. From there he

MacQuitty inspecting the 1905 engines.

The flooding of a boiler room from the film.

deftly manoeuvred lifeboats to their davits, huge lamps to their towers, everything to its correct position.

The canvas we were working to for our story was vast and delicately woven. Roy Baker and I would meet regularly over lunch to talk about our doubts and fears as the film began to develop. At the end of the second week Roy suddenly said that he could clearly see the way ahead. He became supremely confident; the course for *A Night to Remember* was charted. It was our happiest moment. The next set of rushes confirmed his judgement. Roy directed throughout with enormous skill and firmness and kept the actors happy and in balance. Everyone working on the film soon fell under the spell of the ship. It was their film and they were proud of it.

The skills of the plasterers and carpenters were boundless. Nothing, it seemed, was beyond their capabilities. Everything was perfect for the great staircase, the immaculate reproductions of the public rooms, the innumerable mouldings. Sculptors were brought in to help with many of the decorations and also created the miniaturized figures for the final scenes of the sinking. There was one group huddled together in lifebelts as they waited for the end that I had cast in fibreglass.

Although we had decided on a strict documentary approach to every detail, there were two points on which we opted for artistic licence. The first concerned the christening of the ship, for which we laid on a traditional ceremony. Such a thing would have been unheard-of at Harland & Wolff, where they allowed only identification numbers and no champagne. The second liberty we took was with a picture by Wilcockson of Plymouth harbour that had been hung above the smoking room mantelpiece and gone

The christening that did not actually take place at Harland & Wolff.

down with the ship. Instead, with Vetch's agreement, we substituted a copy of *The Entrance to the New World*, by the same artist. After filming was finished I gave the picture to Walter Lord.

Our first-aid medical section was headed by Dr Black and a splendid matron. Fortunately they never had to deal with a serious accident. Every night I went to see if all was well. I was delighted and relieved to be told there had been no casualties. Considering all the loading and lowering of the lifeboats, it was a remarkable record. For those who had to jump over the side, empty cartons were placed twelve feet deep so as to reduce the speed of their falls gradually. No one was ever injured. Feeding the 1,200 workers and innumerable extras, especially at night, was carried out by Pinewood catering staff. They also provided the sumptuous replica meals served to first-class passengers, including a magnificent boar's head. During exterior work on the ship at night everyone could have hot drinks as shooting continued. There was always hot soup, coffee and tea. One of the child actors was Stephen, the son of the comedy actor Arthur Lowe. In the book he wrote about his father, *Arthur Lowe: A Life* (1996), he also recorded his memories of the production:

'Honor Blackman played my Mum, and I had two gorgeous sisters with cherries in their hats and I was in love with both of them. I am indecently proud of the fact that I fell in love so young, and so plurally. A chauffeur-driven car used to collect me and my [real] Mum, who was paid as a chaperone. Sometimes it was an Austin Siddeley, but sometimes it was a Rolls-Royce. It took us to the lot at Pinewood after dark. The scenes on the tilting deck were shot in the evening in winter so everybody's breath would steam.'

Truth to tell

Publicity was all-important. Publicity depended on pictures. The stills photographers used large cameras and arranged movable lamps to suit their subjects. All of this certainly provided the pin-sharp, beautifully composed stills beloved by the cinemas for their front-of-house displays, but it also took up valuable time with interruptions. What was more, we needed realistic shots of the more harrowing scenes. I persuaded John Davis to take the agency for Pentax and Nikon cameras, which would give him a profit besides taking better photographic stills for the film. These cameras had the great advantage of allowing direct focus through the lens, so that what the photographer saw would be what appeared in the print. The small 35mm cameras held thirty-six exposures and were quiet enough to use during the action, nor did they need tripods. They would save us many delays.

Publicity and public relations came under the able leadership of Theo Cowan and his assistant Robert Herrington. They revelled in the unique international material. Bob Herrington was greatly gifted. He took with him everywhere a small briefcase, though no one knew what it had inside it. In fact it contained a sound recorder. I did not like being interviewed and had never been able to work out

Titanic survivor Lawrence Beesley was deeply moved by the re-enactment of the deck scenes.

how Bob managed to write such accurate résumés of meetings and briefings.

Bob Herrington was responsible for the huge information folder, measuring twelve by twenty inches, which had a picture of a newsboy on the cover. It was packed with 105 pages of exploitable background facts, including the film's cast and crew, eyewitness recollections and a list of all the living survivors.

Most of the survivors and descendants with whom we made contact had been glad to be interviewed and many visited the studios and watched rehearsals. Some were overcome by the realism. Captain Smith's daughter was shocked by the remarkable likeness of the actor Laurence Naismith to her father. The former Fourth Officer on the *Titanic*, Commander Joseph Boxhall, was only too delighted to become one of our technical advisers. He had been on deck when the ship struck the iceberg and continued to be at the heart of the rescue operation.

Another highly expert adviser we were lucky to attract to the project was Captain Grattidge, Commodore of the White Star Line and a captain on both the *Queen Mary* and the *Queen Elizabeth*. After the collapse of France in 1940 he had been in charge of the Cunard White Star liner *Lancastria* as it stood off St-Nazaire to evacuate 6,000 troops of the British Expeditionary Force. German dive-bombers

Captain Smith's daughter with actor Laurence Naismith.

managed to drop three bombs on the ship, which keeled over almost immediately and 5,000 soldiers were drowned. So grave was this incident that Churchill, fearing a further

Captain Grattidge (far left), Commodore of the White Star Line and Joseph Boxhall (far right), Fourth officer on the *Titanic* were technical advisers on the set.

collapse of morale in the wake of Dunkirk, suppressed the news for five weeks. Like the *Titanic* tragedy, the *Lancastria* disaster created a survivors' association. Each year on 23 June survivors and their children still attend the annual commemorative service at the church of St Katharine Cree, where a wreath is laid beneath a

stained-glass window that shows Christ walking on the water

One afternoon Genia said, 'There's a Miss Russell on the phone. Can you speak to her now? She says it's most urgent.'

'I've had every disaster but bubonic plague and a husband.'

I knew at once who she was. In the annals of the *Titanic*, Edith Russell was famous as the young woman who owned a lucky musical pig that had been rescued with her, which played the tune 'Maxixe' when its tail was twisted. In his book Walter Lord described how she had used it in the lifeboat to keep children amused. She claimed to be accident-prone. 'I've been in shipwrecks, car crashes, fires, floods and tornadoes,' she was once quoted as saying. 'I've had every disaster but bubonic plague and a husband.' She enjoyed quite a reputation, both in Paris, where she lived,

and New York, for her knowledge of leading fashions. The pig had been given to her as a good-luck charm after a car crash in France. She also claimed to have been the last but one survivor to leave the sinking ship. When a sailor urged her to jump into a lifeboat, she had hesitated till he took the pig she was clutching and threw it in. 'That does it,' she said. 'I'm going after it.'

I took the phone and Edith asked, 'Are you Mr MacQuitty, the producer

of the new *Titanic* film? I said that I was. 'Mr MacQuitty,' she began, 'I can be of great help to you in making this film. I am in the dress business. I have the dress and coat that I wore when the *Titanic* sank. I am an expert. I know what the passengers wore. I would like to be

Edith Russell with the musical pig given to her in 1911.

attached to the costume department. I would also like to help with publicity. I write for many magazines and newspapers. I spend a lot of time in Paris, where I am well-known, and I

Lawrence Beesley (left) giving valuable advice.

can be sure of getting you valuable publicity there. I am in London, staying at the Washington Hotel for two weeks. Can I come and see you at the studio?'

'Please speak to my secretary,' I said, 'and she will fix a date.'

At half past ten one morning, just as I was about to leave the office and go down to the ship, Genia told me that Miss Russell had arrived in reception. 'Ask the photographer to join us,' I told Genia, and went down to meet her. She was a tiny woman, dressed all in black, which accentuated the four strands of large pearls around her neck. She glanced down at her front from time to time, as if to reassure herself that the pearls were still there. Her hair was brown, turning grey. It was plentiful, and beautifully set. She wore no hat nor did I ever see her wearing one.

'Mr MacQuitty, I'm sure glad to see you.' Edith's accent was strong and the pitch of her voice was almost that of a man's.

'And I am delighted to see you,' I said. 'We will go to the ship.'

We walked past the workshops and finally turned a corner to see where a third of the ship rose from its concrete bed. Two funnels, thrust into the winter sky, dwarfed the four lifeboats on the boat deck. Edith stopped in her tracks. She stood still and silent for a long time, until she said, 'I can't believe it.'

Once on the boat deck she took hold of a lifeboat lifeline. Her face was

aged, but strong and determined. Straight eyebrows, set widely apart, enhanced the deep-set eyes. Edith was completely overcome, her thoughts still far away. Quietly the photogra-

Costume sketch for Kate Farrell, steerage passenger; one of the hundreds of sketches drawn for the film by Mardie Madden.

pher took a shot to include the name *Titanic* on the boat. Edith never noticed. Slowly she walked along the deck. 'It was here that I stood,' she said.

We returned to the office. Genia

had tea waiting for us. Suddenly Edith recovered her normal poise. 'Mr MacQuitty,' she announced, 'you've got the ship right, wonderfully right. But the action, what the passengers do and the clothes they wear - that's where you're going to need help and that's where I come in. I want to be attached to this film. I want to check that everything is right. I don't want a lot of money. I will give it to charity, anyway. I intend to leave my musical pig to Walter Lord, and you shall have the clothes that I wore in the lifeboat. What do you say?'

'Miss Russell' I said, 'I am delighted with your interest and appreciation. However, everyone working on the picture is a member of a strict trade union. Even if the studios wished me to employ you I would not be able to. But I am glad to have your advice and will see that you know what is happening.'

Edith was bitterly disappointed at my rejection of the deal she had proposed, and said so in no uncertain terms. Nevertheless the idea of being involved in any capacity was irresistible. 'Mr MacQuitty,' she said, 'on the

Costume design and notes for the *Titanic* uniforms.

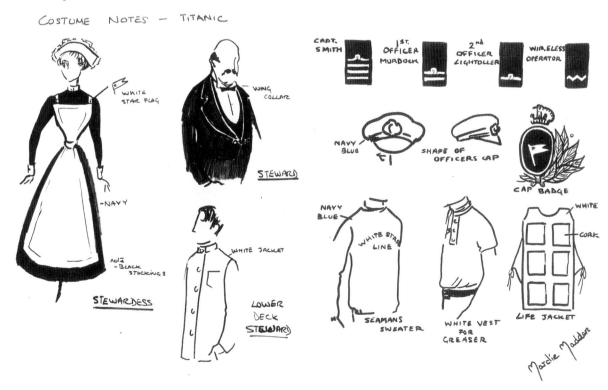

outside you are full of Irish charm, but inside you're a determined, persistent man. Well, I, too, am persistent.'

She now knew and accepted exactly where she stood, and before

Edith Russell became very involved in the filming and her attention to detail was critical.

long we were 'Edith' and 'Bill'. The advice she expressed in simple if forceful language was rewarding, and when the film was shown she, like the rest of the survivors, could find no fault with it. She also played her part in the publicity and found herself in great demand for interviews. She always asked my advice about the fees she was offered. Once the producer of a BBC programme had suggested £15,

saying that was their usual rate. 'But you wouldn't get a dog for £15,' she told him. 'Ah,' he said, 'but at your age do you think you could handle the programme?' 'Then why are you asking me, smarty?' she replied.

A keen money-sense was a constant factor in Edith's life. As Walter Lord recalled, besides the thousands of dollars which she claimed in compensation for her second cabin filled with expensive model gowns that she was taking from Paris to New York, she had also asked for $2 for her hot-water bottle and $20 for face powder and rouge.

One survivor who could never bring herself to watch the filming of *A Night to Remember* was Miss Eva Hart, MBE, JP. Her reason was that the tragedy was still too painful to her and she could not bear to witness its reconstruction. She was seven years old when the *Titanic* began to sink. Her father, a builder who was going to work in Winnipeg, went on deck and quickly recognized the danger. He came back to the cabin, told his wife to dress and wrapped a blanket round Eva's

nightdress before carrying her to the boat deck. After a time she and her mother were helped into Lifeboat 14. Her father's parting words were, 'Stay with your mummy and hold her hand tightly like a good girl.' Eva could never forget how her mother held her close as they had what was to be a last look at her father before the lifeboat dropped below the level of the boat deck. Her mother had felt from the beginning that to claim the boat was unsinkable must be to fly in the face of God's providence.

Despite her reservations, Eva did accept an invitation to the première of the film at the Odeon, Leicester Square. Later she wrote to me. 'I have never been able to bring myself to look at the part where the ship actually sinks. The film itself was so realistic and so well produced that, from my own experience, I was unable to fault anything about it.'

Notes for Individual Action **Fool's paradise for disaster hero**

The story of a man who lived in a fool's paradise for one history-making hour, an hour that was to result in the destruction of a mighty liner, and the deaths of the greater part of her passengers and crew, can now be told … 46 years after it happened.

The man? Quartermaster George Thomas Rowe.

The liner? The doomed *Titanic*.

And SOMEBODY ELSE'S BUNGLING created Rowe's 'paradise'.

Although in a key position, no one told him that the ship was sinking. For a full hour he remained in ignorance of his plight.

Yet he lived to tell the tale.

Memories of that 'lost hour', and the tragic hours that followed are revived by the Pinewood film "A Night to Remember", from the best seller by Walter Lord.

They promise to create a sensation.

Rowe, who lived in Southampton, was on watch on the after bridge when the ship struck the iceberg in mid-Atlantic.

"It had been an uneventful night", he said. "Until I saw what I thought was a windjammer, sails set, gliding close by on the starboard side. Then, almost an hour later I was amazed to see something else follow the same course … A LIFEBOAT!"

Only when he rang the bridge, to report this strange occurrence was Rowe told that the ship had struck, and was holed below the water line.

Only then was he able to react, to play a hero's part in the events of that never-to-be-forgotten tragedy … to help passengers get away and quell minor panics, until, with the ship in her death throes, he was ordered by the Captain to take charge of one of the four collapsibles that carried survivors towards a rescue ship.

In the film, produced by William MacQuitty, directed by Roy Baker, and starring Kenneth More, Rowe is played by actor Cyril Chamberlain.

An extract from the publicity folder for A Night to Remember.

Opening night of the film at the Odeon, Leicester Square, 3rd July 1958.

The final cut

After filming ended, Sidney Hayers, our highly expert editor, produced the final cut and we ran it through. It was the result, linked together, of all our deliberations from watching the rushes that led to finished sequences. Our project had grown from a sapling into a tree. Scene followed scene in a steady flow, moving towards the climax. Nothing felt as if it had been strained or overdone. There was the right proportion of drama and tension. We were confident we had matched our aim to keep within the actual development of the disaster.

Now it needed music to add to the soundtrack. The score would be required to emphasize the power of the largest ship in the world and the challenge of the Northern Atlantic with its icebergs. It must also contrast the luxurious life of the first-class passengers with the situation of those

in steerage. It would have to express the love and sacrifice, the courage and devotion of the wives, children and husbands, and, overall, the terror of a fearful death. William Alwyn was a leading film composer of his generation, besides being a symphonist of note. He had worked on such classics as Carol Reed's *Odd Man Out* as well as on several of my earlier films, and we felt he would be the right choice as composer of the incidental music for *A Night to Remember*.

The orchestra was the Sinfonia of London under the baton of my old friend Muir Matheson, a magical conductor of film music. The secret of his success was an ability to convey his own enthusiasm for a film to the orchestral players. He always worked with the film projected on a large screen behind the orchestra, and each scene was replayed and timed till the interpreta-

tion of the score fitted the mood and action precisely. Muir had a quick, dry Scottish wit and his rehearsals were filled with good humour and skill. I never heard any player resent advice or criticism given in this spirit.

Besides the music, other sound effects were needed, such as the ominous creaking of the doomed vessel. Fortunately these sounds were realistically produced by the groaning and creaking of the sets as they were tilted by the huge hydraulic rams. Fitting in the special sound effects for all the intricate model shots required precise timing. The explosions, the crashing objects, the water rushing - everything demanded total authenticity. Finally, when all the tracks had been successfully blended, the master sound track was added to the picture. The picture was run and re-run, a

'This is the best film we have ever made.'

dissolve here, a small cut there, till finally the release print was born.

The day of reckoning came. The Rank viewing theatre in Wardour Street was turned over to John Davis and his formidable colleagues - those who were responsible for the smooth running and profits of the huge Rank Organization, with its vast network of cinemas at home and abroad. The film was watched in silence. Finally it ended and the lights came up. Everyone waited for John to speak. There was another long silence before he said, 'This is the best film we have ever made.'

It was a moment of great joy for Roy and me. The exhausting work had produced a great film. The most moving image for me had been not one from the film, but of Joseph Boxhall sitting on his own in the theatre as he watched the final scene of the *Titanic* sinking. He had been the officer on deck when the ship struck the iceberg. He had fired the rockets and seen the vessel slowly founder. Had we got it right, I asked him. He wept as he said, 'Terribly right.'

Roy and I were deeply in the debt of Joe Boxhall and the other advisers, who had provided us with an accurate framework for the film. We were also in the debt of all the workers and technicians, who had suffered cold, wet nights to capture reality. None of them had complained. It was as if they had been dealing with a real situation. Many felt they had become part of the ship's company.

The reviews were the best ever received for a product of the Rank Organization

The next step was to prepare for the première. This was arranged to take place at the Odeon Cinema, Leicester Square, on 3 July 1958. It was to be followed by a reception and dinner at the Dorchester Hotel. Important guests received invitations to the cinema, and more important guests to the celebration dinner. No invitations were being sent out to the technicians who had made the film possible.

I called to see John at his headquarters in South Street. He was in a board meeting, but his secretary said he wished me to be present. He intro-duced me cordially to his directors and asked me what I wanted. I replied that I felt that the technical staff and their wives and sweethearts should be invited to the première. Several directors expressed surprise: 'Surely they have seen it already?' 'Of course,' I replied, 'but this is their hour of triumph and naturally they wish to be present.' John gave me a questioning look, but agreed to accommodate them in the stalls.

Usually I felt sad when one of my films was finished, but *A Night to Remember* was a special case, a wonderful, unique experience. It fulfilled a mission for me to tell the story of the *Titanic* whose brief history made such an impression on my life, and to repay some of the debt that I felt I owed her. I went round the departments and thanked the studio staff, who had come together in such an extraordinary way and been profoundly affected. All were proud of the part they had played in the film's creation, from the humblest workers to the top technicians, and seemed to have become part of the great disaster.

Press handout for the first screenings of the film.

R.M.S. TITANIC

Statistics

LAUNCHED	Belfast, 31st May, 1911.
WEIGHT	46,328 gross tons .... 66,000 tons displacement.
LENGTH	882.5 feet.
WIDTH	92.5 feet.
HEIGHT	175 feet from keel to top of funnels (In short; eleven stories high and a sixth of a mile long.)
NO. OF WATERTIGHT COMPARTMENTS	16, all operated electrically from the bridge.
POWER OF ENGINES	50,000 H.P.
MAX. SPEED	24 to 25 knots.
NUMBER OF LIFEBOATS	16 plus 4 collapsibles.
CAPACITY OF LIFEBOATS	1,178.
NO. OF PEOPLE ON TITANIC	2,207.
TITANIC'S CAPTAIN	Edward Smith.

Commenced maiden voyage from Southampton to New York at 12 noon April 10th, 1912 and scheduled to leave Queenstown with 2,208 on board.

Touched at Cherbourg and left for Queenstown at 9 p.m. same day.

One crewman deserts. Titanic leaves Queenstown with 2,207 on board for New York at 2 p.m. April 11th.

Hit iceberg in mid-Atlantic at 11.40 p.m. April 14th.

Sank at 2.20 a.m. April 15th.

PASSENGERS AND CREW – SAVED AND LOST

	MEN		WOMEN		CHILDREN		TOTAL ON BOARD
	SAVED	LOST	SAVED	LOST	SAVED	LOST	
1st CLASS	58	125	139	4	5	1	332
2nd CLASS	13	146	78	15	24	0	276
3rd CLASS	55	398	98	81	23	53	708
CREW	191	677	21	2	–	–	891

(Please note : No two reports on any enquiry give the same total. These figures have been reached after two years' research by the Rank Organisation).

OFFICERS ALIVE IN 1958
3rd officer Pitman...4th officer Boxhall
SURVIVORS TRACED BETWEEN 1955 and 1958 (Not all verified)
UNITED KINGDOM 45 – U.S.A. 40.

TOTAL SAVED – 705   TOTAL ON BOARD – 2,207

It was unusual for a film production to be free from union disputes, but on this occasion they had been absent.

In the Special Effects Department I congratulated Bill Warrington on his well-deserved award for the moving sequence of the sinking ship. He had never, he said, enjoyed his work so much as he had on this film. As I was leaving, he gave me one of the model lifeboats, complete with tiny passengers and electrically controlled oarsmen, a happy memento of his ingenuity.

Now the various shops had to be sorted for work for keeping and work for losing. Everything that had a future use was carefully stored. The unwanted material was consumed in a huge bonfire on the lot. As I watched, more and more familiar pieces of the living scenes we had toiled to produce were thrown into the flames. I shared their end with watering eyes, but I comforted myself with the thought that the effect they created would last as long as the film survived. Finally I finished my goodbyes. It was a strange experience. Part of my life had come to an end, but forty years later its product still exists, frozen in time and ready to be revealed at the touch of a switch.

The première was an astounding success. The film was hailed as one that 'lends new lustre to the British film industry'. The reviews were the best ever received for a product of the Rank Organization. Among the accolades was a letter I received from John Davis:

My Dear Bill,
Some people in this industry can write fulsome letters, but I am afraid I am not one of these people. However I do not want you to think that although this letter is brief it is any the less sincere. May I thank you most sincerely for the great contribution you have made to the making of a great film, *A Night to Remember*. I have watched with pleasure the untiring effort which you have put into this gigantic production and the great organizing work you put in to help the director with his work.
Many thanks.
Yours sincerely,
John

We were still glowing with the tributes when Roy Baker said to me,

Promotional stand in the foyer of the Criterion Theatre on Broadway.

'The door is wide open. We don't even have to push.'

Two days after I received the letter from John Davis, a new Pinewood administrator I had never seen before, Connery Chappel, sent for me. He looked up as I entered his office and offered me a chair. 'The company's not renewing your contract,' he said in a matter-of-fact tone. It expires at the end of this month.' Then he added, because I must have looked puzzled, 'It's company policy and has been ordered by the managing director, John Davis.'

I said nothing. I went back to my office and collected my things. I thanked my devoted secretary, Genia Kaye, for all her support. She was, in any case, going into production. I had joined the ranks of the Rank Outsiders.

When I got home I told Betty. 'When one door closes another opens,' she said.

Convincing the Americans

Betty was proved to be right. In August we were invited to attend a première of *A Night to Remember* in Belfast and the film was a great success there as well. At that time the Independent Television Authority was asking for applications for an independent television franchise in Ulster. We got a group together and we won the contract. I became founding managing director and Betty was my alternate director and later vice-chairman. When I was in the middle of setting up Ulster TV I had a letter from Ken Hargreaves, the president of Rank Film Distributors of America.

Would I spend two weeks in America doing interviews and publicity, he asked - one week in Los Angeles and the other in New York. What was the problem, I asked. It seemed to me that the film spoke for itself. It wasn't just one problem, he replied. The Twentieth Century-Fox picture that had been released in 1953 had two television showings in 1956, which attracted viewing audiences of 46 million. The question being asked in the trade was, 'Why show the story again?' They found the film depressing. It had no American box-office names, since Kenneth More did not rate as a star in the USA. There were no colour stills, whereas all American productions had colour transparencies available, whether a film was in colour

or black and white. These were not only offered to the colour magazines; they were also used all round as a bait for the black and white material to come.

John Davis fully approved of my visit, Ken Hargreaves added. 'Your presence would be of inestimable help in launching the picture publicity-wise.' The publicity that I had achieved for the British release by being available to the press, magazine and broadcasting media, combined with all the other support rounded up by the genius of Theo Cowan and Bob Herrington, had finally struck home.

I arrived in New York on 1 December and was taken to Essex House by Geoffrey Martin, the Rank American publicity chief. 'You have a suite reserved on the top floor,' he told me. I found it had a splendid view of Central Park. It looked down on the ice rink, where many people were skating. We sat in comfortable chairs and raised glasses of Scotch whisky to the success of the picture in America. I took to Geoffrey at once and was impressed by his enthusiasm. He was about forty, full of confidence and good humour, and he loved his job. He was alert to opportunities and got on well with Theo Cowan, who had briefed him on all the possible American contacts and supplied him with everything that might help.

'Bill, I'll be quite frank with you,' Geoffrey began. 'Apart from the importance of your film on the American market for the Rank Organization, it is of paramount importance to me personally. I've been criticised by John Davis for not making the success he imagined out of a whole string of good British pictures. The trouble is, none of them were a *must* for the American market, and let's be honest *A Night to Remember* is not a *must* for the American market either. Nevertheless it is a golden opportunity to place you in the top category of producers, whether in Hollywood or anywhere else.'

We had dinner and talked far into the night on the task that faced me, and the next day I flew to Los Angeles. There I was met by the Rank representative, Steve Edwards, who took charge of everything. All of those who interviewed me were given copies of my CV, compiled by Theo Cowan, and naturally they spent much time grilling me about my life. I had been forewarned that this would happen and managed to link their questions back to the film. All were interested, especially Hedda Hopper, who was allowed an exclusive for her widely syndicated newspaper column, published in 400 newspapers throughout the United States. I was also slotted into a ten-minute ringside

---

Notes for Individual Action **He published a warning**

The story of one of the most startling prophecies ever recorded came to light when the Rank Organisation decided to film the story of the *Titanic* disaster from Walter Lord's book, "A Night to Remember".

Details of the prophecy were used by Walter Lord himself when he started work on his book.

It was discovered that in 1898 a struggling author named Morgan Robertson wrote a novel about a fabulous Atlantic liner, far larger than any that had ever been built.

Robertson packed the ship with rich and complacent people, and then wrecked it one cold April night on an iceberg.

Fourteen years later, a British shipping company built a steamer remarkably like the one in Robertson's novel.

The new liner was 66,000 tons displacement; Robertson's was

70,000 tons. The real ship was 882 feet long; the fictional one 800 feet. Both vessels were triple screw and could make 24-25 knots.

Both could carry about 3,000 people, and both had enough lifeboats for only a fraction of that number. But, then this didn't seem to matter because both were labelled 'unsinkable'.

On April 10th, 1912, the real ship left Southampton on her maiden voyage to New York with a list of passengers whose collective bank balances totalled 250,000,000 dollars. On her way, she too struck an iceberg and went down on a cold April night.

Robertson called his ship the Titan; the British shipping company called its ship the *Titanic* ...

An extract from the publicity folder for A Night to Remember.

interview between bouts at the Los Angeles Wrestling Auditorium.

Forest Lawn, the subject of Evelyn Waugh's novel about American funeral customs, *The Loved One,* was a place I had always wanted to see. The only way that the very tight schedule would allow me to make such a visit, said Steve, was if I agreed to do a phone interview from the embalming room.

'We've had a bit of trouble,' said the director when I got there. 'My chief embalmer has become allergic to the embalming fluid and has been away for weeks. This is bad enough, but many of our clients now arrive in a radioactive condition. Formerly, radioactive needles were withdrawn from the clients, but now radioactive pellets are not removed by the hospitals. Our tables are at the height of the embalmers' genitals, and even with new protective lead shields we may be in trouble.'

At this point Steve came in with the phone. It was time to do my interview. The interviewer asked me how my audience was reacting. 'Quietly,' I said.

With the interview out of the way, I was able to move on to see the funerary makeup department. Here experts worked from photographs to re-create the well-known features. The loved one was then placed in a position preferred by the relatives, perhaps in a familiar chair or sofa, or at a table - whatever they wished. Next came the 'rooms of rest', outside which were red and green lights. If a red light was on, it indicated work in progress. We took a red and discovered a pretty girl coaxing a dimple in a client's cheek, using a needle and thread from inside the mouth.

When all the ministrations were complete, clients were transferred to coffins, ready to take their places in the Halls of Fame with their avenues of vaults. Two bronze flower holders stood on either side of each vault's entrance. Carbon dioxide was circulated around the coffins to discourage

any primitive life forms that might endanger the clients' equilibrium. Burials outside in the park were marked by bronze tablets set so low that the grass could be mowed. The gardens were beautifully laid out, with interesting statuary. A small lake had

Promotional hoarding outside the Criterion Theatre on Broadway.

at its centre a replica of the famous Isle of Innisfree, which mourners could visit in a rowboat if they wished. The hives of the honey bees no longer contained bees, since mourners had been stung in the past, but the bees, continuing a posthumous electronic presence, still buzzed over loudspeakers. As I contemplated the scene, it seemed to me that the ocean grave of the *Titanic* dead was an infinitely preferable prospect and determined that my ashes would be destined for the freedom of the seas.

After I returned to New York, Geoffrey told me over dinner, 'Steve was delighted with your performance. Tomorrow you'll start on a similar round of interviews on the New York circuit.'

The next morning I told the girl in

reception at Essex House that my wife would be arriving to join me in a day's time and asked if I would have to pay extra if she stayed in the suite with me. 'Don't you think you're paying enough already?' she replied. It was one incidental bonus. Rank were paying my expenses, including a first-class seat on the plane, but these did not include Betty's air fare. When she arrived it was a great relief. She was looking wonderful and shared all my problems. We met an old friend, Phillip Burton, whom I had cast in *Blue Scar,* my film made on location in South Wales in the 1940s, using real coal mines and miners. Phillip was head of BBC Wales at the time, and he had begged me to let his adoptive son, Richard, have a part. Alas, the only role suitable was already signed up with another actor. This must make me the only producer in film history to have turned down Richard Burton. For the press reception drink and canapés were lavishly laid on. Geoffrey was in his element and delighted with the level of

This must make me the only producer in film history to have turned down Richard Burton

attendance. Betty received a warm welcome and talked to everyone she met with a keen interest. I had not expected it to be such a friendly, informal affair. Then I was told the likely reason. A newspaper strike in New York was unfortunately coinciding with the press showing of the film. It was the first I had heard of it; I had been far too preoccupied with everything else to catch up on this piece of news. I felt overwhelmed. We were going to all this trouble for nothing. Strike or no strike, said the press, they still had to send in their copy if they wanted to be paid. I therefore talked to them about the various adverse opinions we had been hearing from those who had not yet seen the picture, and felt I had at least made the argument that these criteria could not really be applied to a film that set out to present the facts as they actually occurred.

For his part, Geoffrey was not at all discouraged once they had left and seemed satisfied with the results. 'They will give accurate reviews,' he said, 'they are professionals, but they do not expect the American public to accept this British film.' I sensed from the beginning that they had been deeply impressed by what I had to say, but there had been no way for me to convince them that the film might attract American audiences. 'Tomorrow you'll have another busy day,' said Geoffrey.

Next morning I was being interviewed in a television studio by a confident lady who had the CV Theo Cowan had prepared for me in front of her. As she went through my life, she especially relished the parts which gave her the chance to become deeply invasive. In those days, chat shows in America seemed to have no fixed finishing point, but continued as long as an interviewer felt an audience could be held. Twenty minutes went by without any mention of the film, so

I broke the spell by interjecting a remark about American prejudices against British films and then launched into my oft-repeated pitch, maintaining that it was the ship that was the star.

A Night to Remember opened for a week on 16 December at the Criterion Theatre on Broadway on a roadshow basis. It was a small theatre and its entrance was hemmed in by a road-

William MacQuitty, Walter Lord and
Dr J William Stitt at the US gala performance.

repair job with a clutter of trestles and debris. The outlook seemed pretty grim to me. 'We are lucky to get a week,' Geoffrey reassured me brightly. 'Every theatre is booked up with films to 31 December so they will qualify for the April awards.'

The opening was given as a benefit for a charity and many big names in the movies turned up and were duly interviewed. Some of the American survivors were photographed with Walter Lord and when the film ended there was applause.

Betty and I returned to the suite at Essex House conscious of the fact that, while we shared a common language with Americans, there were formidable differences between our two peoples. Next morning we made our farewells with Geoffrey Martin and Ken Hargreaves and flew to Nassau for a

much-needed holiday. By the time we got to New York before flying home again there was a pilots' strike. An elderly captain left his office desk to be our pilot, and because of the strike and the freezing conditions we had to board the plane while it was still in its hangar. There was much confusion. Betty disappeared into the crowded economy section while I joined the queue for first class. After an alarmingly bumpy long run we took off and climbed into quieter weather. As soon as the seatbelt indicators were turned off I went to look for Betty. To my surprise we met in the aisle. 'My seat didn't work,' she said 'so the kindly captain, who was doing his social round, moved me into first class. He said it was shame you didn't give me your seat!'

It was gratifying to receive in due course a copy of the memorandum Steve Edwards sent to Ken Hargreaves summarizing the results of the promotion campaign in Los Angeles. I had made a 'splendid impression' on the media, he wrote. 'His presentation of his subject was masterful and eloquent giving at all times his interviewers and listeners a clear understanding of the importance of

when the film ended there was applause

A Night to Remember as a motion picture production. The interest ... is best explained by the fact that his time on camera or on the air far exceeded the usual time allotted to guest appearances.' I had been guest on nine television programmes in three days and given three radio interviews. The value of the Hedda Hopper interview was reckoned in many thousands of dollars. Apart from my own efforts, interviews with survivors on their reactions to the film had been well publicized and had helped to convince people about our claims to realism and authenticity of approach.

Probing the depths

Today the Americans, like the rest of the world, accept *A Night to Remember* on its merits as a classic cinematic account of the story of the *Titanic*. From the outbreak of the First World War in 1914 up till the release of the film in 1958, there had been little interest in the ship. Even Hitler considered the German version made as anti-British propaganda during the Second World War to be too alarming and thought it might have a counter-productive effect with the German people. Even with *A Night to Remember* relatively few people went to see it initially. It had no stars; how could a ship be a star?

Then, in the early 1960s, a remarkable event took place and the mood changed almost overnight. Edward Kamuda, a jeweller in Indian Orchard, Pennsylvania, formed a group of like-minded enthusiasts and started the Titanic Historic Society. The society was an instant success. It had an almost religious impact, like an enlightenment. More societies followed its example and spread over the years till *Titanic* societies came to circle the globe.

No one was more delighted than Walter Lord or myself. Our belief in the timeless qualities in the story had been vindicated. The societies in the United States, where the scepticism had been greatest, were the most committed of all. Members gathered to celebrate the last dinner menu, and survivors and the relatives of those who had been lost came into contact with each other to help with keeping memories of the event alive.

As artefacts and memorabilia with *Titanic* connections began to be collected, so their sale-room prices rocketed. In 1980, when we moved from a rambling house in the country to a compact flat above the River Thames, we realized there would not be room for half our belongings and sent the surplus to auction. Included in the sale was the model lifeboat given me by Bill Warrington. It fetched £67. Eighteen years later the same model was resold for £3,600.

One day a young man came to see me to discuss an idea he had to buy the insurance covering the wreck. Once he owned the wreck, he said, he would be able to raise it by flotation. The result was that many schemes were suggested, among them a plan to freeze the water around the wreck so that it would rise to the surface in a huge block of ice. But the first step was to find the wreck. This was achieved by Robert Ballard's group in 1985.

The discovery of the site set up a storm of protest. Bob Ballard himself said that it must not be disturbed. The ship was the grave of all those who had died that night and must be left in peace and not desecrated by looters. Eva Hart, as one the survivors, was determined to stop any attempts to take artefacts from the wreck. For her it was sacred to the memory of the dead, her father among them. Walter and I, on the other hand, thought it unlikely that anyone had actually gone down with the ship. One of the apparent puzzles to do with the sinking was the discrepancy between the number of bodies recovered and the number of those never found. The total of those known to be aboard who were never accounted for was 1,186. Some clues to this may be contained in a letter written by Francis Dyke, a wireless telegraphy operator, to his mother from the cable ship *Minia* which was one of the four search vessels:

May 2nd
Being again on watch it is now 3a.m. I will write a little more. We have been sailing about looking for bodies for the last four days and have only picked up seventeen. There has been a lot of wind and bad weather since the accident so the bodies are much scattered. Some we picked up over 130 miles from the wreck as they go very fast when in the Gulf Stream.

The ship had broken apart as she went down and most of the wreckage they came across was from below deck, including pieces of the grand staircase. One way or another, the bodies must have been scattered into the seas and often carried far by the currents, to be dispersed before long by the attentions of fish and gulls. To think of the *Titanic* as a marine grave was therefore a misconception. We also felt that if no salvage was allowed, then all the relics would be lost and soon forgotten again.

There were months of wrangling at

the end of which the wreck was acquired by RMS Titanic Inc., a company set up for that purpose. Its founders were Arnie Geller and George Tulloch, who were dynamos of energy and unbounded in their determination to salvage the wreck. The company contracted with the US government that the artefacts would never be sold, but instead be lent to museums so that the world could appreciate the tragedy. In 1987 George arranged for two cruise liners to take 1,800 people to the wreck site to watch on underwater TV as the French submergible *Nautile* attached floats to a twenty-ton piece containing six portholes that had broken from the ship's side and lay at the bottom. Unfortunately, just as the piece reached the surface, it broke away and returned to the depths. Undaunted, George raised it successfully the following year.

The never-ending voyage

Those of us involved in making the film of *A Night to Remember* had little idea at the time how much we were intertwining our lives with the legend of the *Titanic* as it continued to unfold. To me one of the most rewarding outcomes had been in the area of friendship - with Walter Lord and, above all, with two of the survivors, Edith Russell and Eva Hart.

Edith maintained an enormous interest in living and was full of charitable works. She fought long battles with the French authorities to get better conditions for the wild birds in their cramped cages in the Paris bird market. Finally she gave up Paris, leaving eight trunks in store in the Hôtel Lutetia, which had been the German headquarters during the war, and moved to London. She spent her Christmases with us, as a family. She always brought presents for the children and loved getting hers off the tree. Sometimes she would doze, but covered up for this by saying that she never listened when other people talked.

In the case of Eva Hart, her mother had made the decision to bring her home to England on the *Celtic* when it sailed on 29 April 1912. Eva became an intelligent, talented young woman, with a fine singing voice and a pressing desire to help others. She took a job as welfare officer to the Sterling Engineering Company and remained with them for twenty-five years. After a change of management ended her employment, she started her own company, which she found more enjoyable. She was in great demand as a talented singer and courageously overcame her reluctance to talk about the events of the *Titanic* disaster. In fact she was known world wide as one of the few survivors who could speak clearly and fearlessly about that terrible night. More than anything she loved her voluntary work, which included being a lay magistrate as well as involvement with family planning and the Women's Royal Voluntary Service (WRVS). Of receiving the MBE in 1973 she wrote: 'I had never thought that the work I did so willingly and from which I derived so much satisfaction and

---

Notes for Individual Action **Beginning and end of the mighty Titanic**

The mystery of seven and a half lost hours after the mighty R.M.S. *Titanic* sank in mid-Atlantic is recalled by Pinewood's "A Night to Remember".

From mid-day on April 15th, 1912, to 7.30 pm that night, the world believed the *Titanic* was still afloat and that all lives had been saved.

Who was responsible for the radio message which flashed between world capitals has never been discovered. The exact movements of the great liner are listed below:

1909 - Keel laid at Belfast

1911 - May 31st. The vessel is launched and named *Titanic*.

1912 - Completed and fully furnished at cost of approximately two million pounds.

April 10th

Mid-day. Started on maiden trip from Southampton to New York via Cherbourg.

April 14th

Sent out routine radio message of presence of icebergs off the Grand Banks of Newfoundland.

11.40 pm: *Titanic* strikes an iceberg at latitude 41.16 north, Longitude 50.14 west.

Midnight. *Carpathia* and other vessels hear *Titanic's* call for help.

About 1.00 am: First news reaches U.S.A. via Montreal that *Titanic* has struck an iceberg.

April 15th

2.20 am: *Titanic* sinks.

4.10 am: First boat of survivors picked up by Carpathia.

Mid-day: Reports reach New York that *Titanic* is still afloat and all saved.

7.30 pm: Shipping line admits a great loss of life.

April 16th

Carpathia sends radio message giving list of survivors.

April 18th

9.30 pm: *Carpathia* docks at New York with 705 survivors and first details of *Titanic* disaster.

An extract from the publicity folder for *A Night to Remember*.

pleasure would receive such recognition.'

For years I tried to persuade Eva to write her autobiography, but she was totally opposed to the idea. There came a time when she was suffering from the loss of a kneecap and other serious conditions that required frequent spells in hospital. Fortunately she then made up her mind to tell her life story to her great friend, a forensic scientist Ronald C. Denney. The book, *Shadow of the Titanic A Survivor's Story* (1994), had a picture of a doll's head, retrieved from the wreck, on the cover. It was beautifully written and took its place at once among the most important *Titanic* memoirs.

The last time I saw Eva was on Saturday, 15 April 1995, at the opening of the Memorial Garden of Remembrance in the gardens of the National Maritime Museum at Greenwich, where a plain monument carved from Cornish granite recalled those who were lost on the *Titanic*. Eva was there to take part in the simple but emotional ceremony with another survivor, Edith Haisman, both of them now in wheel chairs. Eva and I spoke of the old days and of all that her association with the *Titanic* had meant to her in its most positive aspects. It seemed to me that one of the rewards for the survivors' tragic suffering had been an ability to face life with sympathy and impressive courage. Eva died less than a year later, aged ninety-one. When Ronald Denney said, 'Someone who has such a huge spirit leaves a great gap,' I could not have agreed with him more.

Inevitably time has continued to gather up all those who had direct links with the tragedy, but Edith Haisman was still able to come with a group of us on the TSS *Island Breeze* at the end of August 1996 when we sailed to take part in a memorial service above the wreck, when Betty and I threw wreaths on to the water. Another survivor who was with us on this occasion was Michel Navratil, who was only a small boy when his father handed him and his brother Edmond into one of the lifeboats. For a while there was confusion about their identity because Monsieur Navratil was travelling under the assumed name of 'Hoffman', having kidnapped his sons from his estranged wife to take them to America. They were happily reunited with their mother, but while their father's body was one of those recovered, he was buried in the Jewish cemetery by mistake.

Walter Lord continues to be an honoured guest at *Titanic* functions and, despite being confined to a wheel chair and needing a special attendant, he came to London for the première of the Canadian director James Cameron's film *Titanic*. We had not seen each other for several years and, with my whole family, we spent many happy hours reliving the past and wondering about the future, especially since the surge of interest in the *Titanic* appeared to be continuing indefinitely. Undoubtedly the new film was having an enormous effect. There were those who complained that it was not a true account of the disaster but it was never intended to be. The purpose of James Cameron's *Titanic* was to tell an epic love story within the context of a calamity, and he had made the most successful box-office film the world has yet seen. Scenes that made the drama stronger were essential to this approach. Cameron arranged to have the ship sunk horizontally so that the rising waters could be shown bursting along the corridors below deck as the passengers struggled against them. In fact we know that the waters rose slowly, inch by inch; a far less dramatic effect.

When I spoke to James Cameron I told him that he had fashioned a projectile that had hit its target. It was a description he liked. In return he told me that he had a wonderful experience with the Russian crews of the submergibles used to get the location shots of the wreck. They were a very tough lot and to them this was just another of the endless wrecks they dived on to. One night he showed them *A Night to Remember*. When they came out many were weeping.

I told James that we had shared one problem in common. 'What was that?' he asked.

'Getting the money, I replied. 'I had to raise half a million pounds and you had to raise $230 million.' We both laughed, and I continued, 'You had one great advantage. You had computers. I had to do everything mechanically.'

'And what a wonderful film you produced,' he said. 'I made great use of it and of Walter's book.'

At the close of the twentieth century we live in a rapidly changing world. Harland & Wolff make fewer ships, but are happily involved in encouraging and promoting hundreds of *Titanic* replicas, uniforms, badges - anything that will sell. Recently I received a catalogue from the Titanic Leisurewear Corporation: 'Their Autumn & Winter Merchandise. The ONLY UK Company licensed to sell Titanic clothing by Harland & Wolff.'

The Ulster Titanic Society was a late starter in the field, but after only six years they promoted a Titanic Celebration Week hosted by the Lord Mayor of Belfast. It was supported by the older societies and many international celebrities. It was a huge success and encouraged many further projects. The Japanese are considering building a full-sized replica *Titanic* as a hotel on the site of the dockyards and Ulster plans to build a museum, possibly on the original slipway to house artefacts and memorabilia. The new chairman of the Ulster society, Stephen Cameron, has written a unique book, *Belfast's Own Titanic*, about the men who built the ship, and Harland &

'I had to raise half a million pounds and you had to raise $230 million.'

Wolff have struck a bronze medal to commemorate the *Titanic*. One of the few aspects of the story not covered by any book so far was the making of the film *A Night to Remember*. When I discussed the idea that I should write one with my excellent editor Peter Ford, he asked, 'Why another book on the *Titanic*? You have made a matchless film. Why not leave it at that?' I replied, 'All the people who made the film should be remembered for their superb work and Pinewood Studios for their superb support. The story's part of my life. It helped me, and it might help others.' The new *Titanic* film had also renewed interest in the problems faced by myself and James Cameron as producers.

I am frequently asked why James Cameron's latest version of the story has taken such a hold on its audiences and why *A Night To Remember* has come to be so revered by so many. I reply that it is because every section of society can associate with someone on board. Part of the fascination is, I think, that audiences participate in the disaster. Perhaps they wonder how they would act in similar circumstances. In reality, more than 1,500 people died, most of them mercifully in less than twenty minutes. The killing cold did its work quickly. But the members of the audiences all know that they too must die in time and could face an even grimmer fate. Hopefully the film in either version may give them courage.

The original disaster certainly confirmed my belief that life is for living as fully as possible. Lost opportunities do not return. 'Too late' are the saddest words in any language. Time is our most precious gift. Our wonderful world may not appeal to everyone, and using time to its best advantage is difficult though this was never a problem for any of the *Titanic* survivors that I met. The thing they had in common was a keen sense of living and making the most of their lives. They all had a calm, appreciative outlook, they cherished their friends and they enjoyed themselves.

When I wrote my autobiography *A Life to Remember* (1991) I received a flood of letters wanting to know how I managed to do so many different things. In answer I wrote another book, *Survival Kit: How to Reach Ninety and Make the Most of it* (1996). This stated my belief that between our ears is a vast storehouse of inherited knowledge that has brought us safely through hostile environments for millions of years. Nature is the power that rules the universe, and the fate of the *Titanic* was a clear signal that human arrogance needs to be humbled if our species is to continue on a course of survival. Death is the positive yardstick for living that gives our lives meaning and purpose.

The following pages are reproduced from the UK publicity brochure for the film.

The Rank Organisation presents with pride

enneth More in **A NIGHT TO REMEMBER**

THE RANK ORGANISATION PRESENTS WITH PRIDE

Kenneth More

in

A NIGHT
TO
REMEMBER

From the book by Walter Lord

Screenplay by Eric Ambler   *Produced by* William MacQuitty   *Directed by* Roy Baker

MADE AT PINEWOOD STUDIOS IN LONDON, ENGLAND   EXECUTIVE PRODUCER EARL ST. JOHN.

THE PLAYERS

Lightoller	Kenneth More	Mrs. Brown	Tucker McGuire	Victualling Manager	Richard Hayward
Mr. Clarke	Ronald Allen	Lucas	John Merivale	3rd Steward	Thomas Heathcote
Peuchen	Robert Ayres	Yates	Ralph Michael	Polish Mother	Danuta Karell
Mrs. Lucas	Honor Blackman	Captain Smith	Laurence Naismith	Engineer Officer Hesketh	Andrew Keir
Captain Rostron	Anthony Bushell	Captain Lord	Russell Napier	Polish Girl	Christina Lubicz
Murphy	John Cairney	Hoyle	Redmond Phillips	Gibson	Barry MacGregor
Mrs. Clarke	Jill Dixon	Joughin	George Rose	Steward No. 5	Eddie Malin
Mrs. Lightoller	Jane Downs	Dr. O'Loughlin	Joseph Tomelty	Mr. Farrell	Patrick McAlinney
Col. Gracie	James Dyrenforth	Sir Richard	Patrick Waddington	Mrs. Straus	Helen Misener
Andrews	Michael Goodliffe	Boxhall	Jack Watling	Kate	Mary Monahan
Phillips	Kenneth Griffith	Evans	Geoffrey Bayldon	Lowe	Howard Pays
Lady Richard	Harriette Johns	Moody	Michael Bryant	Clergyman (Carpathia)	Philip Ray
Chairman	Frank Lawton	Q.M. Rowe	Cyril Chamberlain	Stone	Harold Siddons
Murdoch	Richard Leech	Gallagher	Richard Clarke	Mr. Bull	Julian Somers
Bride	David McCallum	Mrs. Farrell	Bee Duffell	Groves	Tim Turner
Cottam	Alec McCowen	Guggenheim	Harold Goldblatt	Mr. Straus	Meier Tzelniker
		3rd Officer (Carpathia)	Gerald Harper		

Production Controller for Pinewood Studios	Arthur Alcott	Production Manager	Jack Hanbury	Hairdresser	Pauline Trent
		Assistant Director	Robert Asher	Sound Editor	Harry Miller
Music composed by	William Alwyn	Camera Operator	David Harcourt	Sound Recordists	Geoffrey Daniels
Played by	Sinfonia of London	Continuity	Penny Daniels		Gordon K. McCallum
Conducted by	Muir Mathieson	Costume Designer	Yvonne Caffin	Special Effects	Bill Warrington
Director of Photography	Geoffrey Unsworth B.S.C.	Make Up	W. T. Partleton	Set Dresser	Len Townsend
Art Director	Alex Vetchinsky			Stills Photographs by	Norman Gryspeerdt
Editor	Sidney Hayers				

The Unsinkable TITANIC...!

On April 10th, 1912, Titanic, the liner they said was unsinkable, sailed from Southampton. At 11.40 p.m. on April 14th, she struck an iceberg and sank within three hours. Fifteen hundred of her 2,207 passengers and crew were drowned. Millionaires who had paid £870 for their passage, and steerage passengers who had paid £8, died together in the ice-cold Atlantic. This film is the true story of that disaster.

The Last Word in Luxury

Titanic was the last word in sea-going luxury when she sailed on her first and last voyage. There was even the novelty of a Turkish bath on board. While steerage accommodation was austere, the millionaires, titled travellers and other first class passengers were given the luxuries they were accustomed to expect ashore. Their private suites and cabins were elaborately furnished in the ornate style of the Edwardian period; menus which were the creations of famous chefs were served to them as they sat in the richly carpeted, palm-decked dining room. Titanic was a small town at sea, eleven storeys high and a sixth of a mile long.

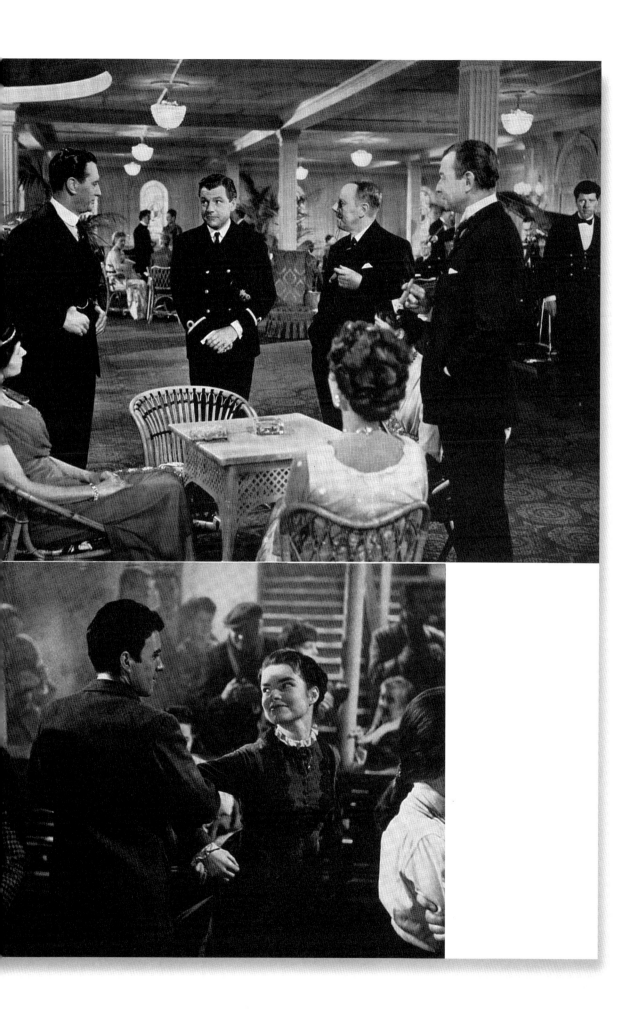

TITANIC Was Doomed

Through the afternoon and evening of April 14th, Titanic's radio kept picking up ice warnings. Suddenly there was tension . . . "Iceberg dead ahead!" . . . engine-room bells shrilled; the wheel spun to starboard. Wet and glistening, the berg loomed closer, towered over the ship, scraped along her side. Then it was gone, leaving a mortal gash, 300 feet long, below the waterline. Titanic was doomed.

She Can't Stay Afloat "

It was difficult, at first, to understand that there could possibly be any real danger. " But she can't sink: she's unsinkable," protested Captain Smith when Thomas Andrews, who built Titanic, told him quietly that nothing could stop his ship from being carried down by sheer weight of water pouring in from below decks.

" It's a mathematical certainty," replied Andrews. " With that amount of underwater damage, she can't stay afloat."

She can't stay afloat. . . .

Only the stokers, firemen and greasers understood the danger as they watched the grey waters swirl higher and higher in the boiler-room.

" Really," protested a mildly indignant lady passenger when told to wear her lifebelt and go on deck, " It's too tiresome. Everybody knows this ship can't sink."

But Titanic couldn't stay afloat. She was already settling, bows-down, into the ice-calm waters of the Atlantic.

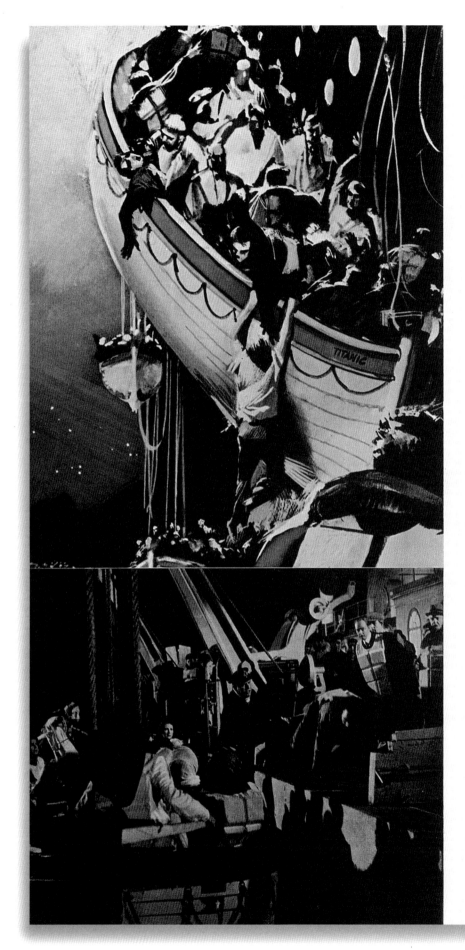

"Women and
Children First"

It wasn't a shouted command to splinter the night with drama: it was spoken quietly and calmly by the bearded Captain Smith. But even as the crew began shepherding the women and children into the lifeboat, there were many who protested that it wasn't necessary. "In a small boat like that?" said one woman. "I can't go without my husband." An angry lady wrapped in chinchilla flatly refused to take her place. She would, she said, catch her death of cold.

But realisation at last began to catch up with facts. One of four men calmly playing cards in the smoking room noticed that the whisky in his glass was not level with the rim. Titanic was slowly settling down by the bows.

There was a "swoosh" as a distress rocket arched into the starlit sky. Momentarily it showed up the strained faces of the officers and crew—the bewilderment of the passengers huddling on deck puzzled to know whether the danger was urgent enough to make them face the cold terrors of an open lifeboat after the comfort of Titanic.

It alarmed the emigrants in their austere quarters in the steerage. They began to clamour for access to the boat deck. Fear gave them the courage to break down any barriers in their way to a chance of safety. Safety? With more than two thousand, two hundred people on board and space in the lifeboats for only twelve hundred? Safety indeed!

As Titanic's stern rose higher, the hesitancy gave place to a rush for places in the boats . . . the rush to a scramble. A surge of steerage passengers stabbed the night with panic. . . .

Titanic's wireless sent out ceaseless appeals for help.
Fifty-eight miles away, the liner Carpathia picke[d]
them up and headed for the scene. But she woul[d]
take four hours, and Titanic had only a short tim[e]
to live.

The Ship That Watched

Ten miles away, the crew of the cargo ship Californian saw the lights of Titanic. They saw her stop—'for safety', they thought, for Californian herself had stopped because of field ice ahead. They watched the distress rockets arc into the sky. 'Company signals,' they decided. Her captain tried to contact the liner with lamp signals. There was no reply. And so, throughout the night, Californian watched, unknowing, the greatest peace-time sea disaster of the century. It was not until the dawn that she knew, and then it was too late to help.

A Hymn Floated Over the Water

Every lifeboat had gone, but there were still 1,500 people left in Titanic. As her bows dipped beneath the icy waters, passengers and crew fought their way to the stern, now rising higher and higher out of the sea. For a few moments there was a hush as a violin was heard playing a hymn. One by one, other instruments of the ship's orchestra joined in. Then one of Titanic's huge funnels fell. The liner reared up like a black finger pointing to the starlit sky, paused and slid down into her grave. A thin, smoky vapour soiled the clear night.

Producer's Diary (highlights)

PRODUCER	William MacQuitty ('Q')
DIRECTOR	Roy Baker
SCRIPTWRITER	Eric Ambler
CAMERAMAN	Geoff Unsworth
ART DIRECTOR	A. Vetchinsky
P.M.	Jack Hanbury
EDITOR	Sid Hayers
COSTUME DESIGNER	Yvonne Caffin
CONTINUITY	Penny Daniels

1956 June

Synopsis received from J.B.

Book "A Night to Remember" (Walter Lord) requested from Story Dept.

Memo to J Briggs, James Archibald and Earl St.John suggesting that film is made.

1956 September

'Q' has meeting with J.M.A. it is agreed to make "A NIGHT TO REMEMBER" commencing approx. Sept. 1957.

'Q' has script lunch with Eric Ambler.

Draft script received from E.A.

1957 February

Walter Lord's comments on draft script received.

1957 March

Semi - final script received.

'Q' and Walter Lord met at Odeon, Leicester Sq. and lunched at the 'Hungaria' with party of 40 (including 14 survivors).

1957 May

Model of "OLYMPIC" arrives, on loan from Liverpool Museum.

1957 June

E.A. comes to Pinewood for script conference.

E. Stage to be used for stateroom sets, dimensions (in feet): 882½ x 92½ x 60½.

1957 July

Because of Model Work and B.P. (back projection) this picture should be shot on normal 35mm. B & W. stock. There is at present no high speed Vista Vision Camera for model work. Also there is available library stock in 35mm. which would not match in with Vista Vision.

Vetch to proceed with possible locations and methods for shooting the lowering of the life boats, and the life boats in the water. R.Q.

The Budget Dept. will expect a schedule and breakdown by the middle of August if they are to prepare their budget in time for the picture to start at the beginning of October.

UNIT – The following Unit has been allocated:

DIRECTOR	Roy Baker
PRODUCTION MANAGER	Jack Hanbury
CAMERAMAN	Eric Unsworth
ART	Vetchinsky
COSTUMES	Yvonne Caffin
PUBLICIST	Bob Herrington
FIRST ASSISTANT	Bob Asher
STILLS	Norman Gryspert
CONTINUITY	Shirley Barnes

(Requested by Kenneth More)

'Q' writes to Victor Finney requesting information on various launchings.

Script conference - E.A. RB. A.V. 'Q'

Jackson Wolf, Barrister, 11a, New Square, London W.C.2.

'Q' and R.B. see German version of 'TITANIC' at National Film Archive Theatre.

Script meeting with WMacQ, RB. EA. in London.

Mr Gill (Baltic Shipping Co.) Visits Pinewood (R.B. JH)

'Q' lunches with Reg. Holmes (Vickers)

Meeting 'Q's office to discuss models, ways of shooting, lowering of lifeboats etc. (R.B. A.V. JH. WW.)

1957 August

Final script received.

Meeting re Music - WmacQ. Muir Matheson, Wm. Alwyn. (Pinewood)

Viewing 15 min. Newsreel of Titanic (Film Institute)

'Q' and RB. lunch with Kenneth More at Shepperton.

'Q' visits P. & O. and sees Malcolm Miller (morning)

'Q' visits Hon. Co. of Master Mariners (afternoon)

Capt. Grattidge assigned as Tech. Adviser.

Col. Lightoller visits 'Q' at Pinewood.

RB. JH. AV. to Inverkeithing, Liverpool and Barrow in Furness, to see Franconia, Largs Bay etc.

Capt. Grattidge lunches with 'Q' at Pinewood. 'Atlantic Night' and Globe Newsreel viewed.

'Q' RB. JH. AV. Visit Capt. Meyer (Shaw Savill) at Royal Albert Dock, and inspect "MV.Dominion Monarch"

Casting Conference in 'Q's office ('Q'. Drury, RB. JH. Continuity)

J.D. approves budget (success!)

Unit view 'Atlantic Night' (American), library material - icebergs, ships' sirens etc.

1957 September

Casting Conference

JD. Writes to 'Q'

'Q' approached by Olga Springfellow ('Daily Express') per phone.

Unit view 20th Century Fox Titanic Film, and German Titanic Film.

Capt. Grattidge visits Pinewood

Unit views German version of Titanic

Meeting in 'Q's office with Model Makers, RB. AV. WW.

H.H.Mumby (wife and son) of T.W.Ward, Sheffield, visits Pinewood.

T.V. version (16mm) A.N.T.R. viewed in Tunnel.

Jympson Harman (Evening News) phones 'Q' re A.N.T.R.

Unit views 'ATLANTIC'.

Kenneth More (with 'Q', Capt.Grattidge and YC) for fitting at Morris Angel,

Capt. Grattidge and Bob Herrington visit Commdr. Boxhall.

JH. AV. LT. Visit Royal Albert Dock

Capt.Meyer (Shaw Savill Line) visits Pinewood, also Cpt. Grattidge

RB. JH. AV. Visit Royal Albert Docks

Pre-Production meeting.

Casting at South Street

Commander Boxhall & Mrs Boxhall visit Pinewood, also Capt. Grattidge.

R.A.Hodson (Manager, Shaw Savill & Albion) phones to say his firm wishes to withdraw their offer of facilities for shots on DOMINION MONARCH or any other of their ships.

'Q' contacts Ship Breaking Industries, Garelochhead re the ASTURIAS. It is proposed that RB. GU. AV. and JH. go up on Friday (this day) to inspect the ship. Inspection successful.

1957 October

Shooting commences on location at Ruislip Lido.

Shooting commences in Studio.

2nd Unit to Gairelochhead to shoot on ASTURIAS.

Col. Lightoller and his mother (Mrs Lightoller) visit studio and meet "CAPT.SMITH" on the set.

1957 November

Corres.in M'chester Guardian by 'Q' on Rebbeck of H & Wolff's criticism of film.

Capt.Shorter & party visit studio.

Pictures of Titanic model appear in local press, in corres: which ensues it is decided to exploit the unwelcome publicity. ('Q' interviews Roberts of Shawcraft).

F.Dent - Ray (survivor Steward) and wife visit studio. Interview with 'Q' tape-recorded.

John Aldridge (B.B.C.Manchester) interviews RB. KM. and David McCallum.

Francis Russell Flint receives £50.advance on his fee for painting series of pictures for A.N.T.R.

1957 December

KM. lunching with Herrington and Ruth Morgan of 'WOMAN', at Pinewood.

KM. visits offices of 'Woman'.

Edith Russell & Dr.Lederman visit Pinewood.

S.E.Daniels (3rd Cl.Steward) & Mrs Daniels visit Pinewood.

Mr & Mrs V.Waddington visit Pinewood.

Night shooting on Lot commences.

Memo form ESJ. saying that JD feels the deck scenes on Carpathia look obviously 'studio' - reshoot ??

1958 January

Night shooting continued.

Mr & Mrs Collins (Hill,Mennim) visit set.

Beesley (survivor) daughter and grandson visit set (as RB's guests)

S.Fallon advises budget £5000. over.

F.Russell Flint signs contract.

Miss Jessup(surviving stewardess) phones Q from London and tells him she has read in an East Anglian paper that A.N.T.R. has been postponed. Q. tells her she has been misinformed.

Q is interviewed by Roy Bradford(B.B.C.) for broadcast on Northern Ireland Station on 4 Feb.

1958 February

A.C.Gardiner of Shipbreaking Industries and Mr. Machonochie of Marconi visit Pinewood.

Robt.Herrington informs Q that to date A.N.T.R. has averaged 24.2ft column inches per week in national and provincial press and magazines.

Mr. Beesley (survivor) visits night set to advise on the 'screams' of the victims.

Edith Russell and party also visit.

Sir Robt. and Lady Grandsen(N.Ireland Agent) visit Pinewood and dine with Q.

Letter from Richard Hayward requesting material and stills suitable for articles he has been asked to write for the Irish press (passed to RH)

Memo from M.M.Stanley - Evans advising that JD. wishes A.N.T.R. to be delivered on 30 May (Three weeks ahead of estimated date). Q.arranged meeting with members of unit concerned.

Cmdr.Boxhall interviewed by Craddock of B.B.C.

Meeting with Sid Hayers, John Dennis, Harry Miller Bill Girdlestone (Denham), Jack Hanbury to discuss ways of improving delivery date.

Revised delivery schedule sent to M.M.S - Evans with ccs. to ESJ. CC. AA. John Dennis.

DELIVERY DATE - 6 JUNE.

1958 March

Last day of shooting (4th March).

Running rough cut for Muir Mathieson etc.

End of Production Party

J.D. E.S.J. and CC. see rough cut of A.N.T.R.

Eric Ambler lunches with Q. at Pinewood (Discuss additional scene etc.)

Q. entertains the Bott family to lunch (they afforded facilities for the Egham location).

1958 April

Q. does recording at South Street for overseas publicity.

John Oldham (friend of Ismay family) and Mr & Mrs Dent Ray visit Q. re portrayal of Ismay.

1958 July

Première at the Odeon Cinema, Leicester Square (3 July).

1958 December

Première at the Criterion Theatre, New York City (16 December).